Why Yo

Derek Doepker

MW00877018

DerekDoepker.com

Facebook.com/DerekDoepkerPage

Twitter.com/ExcuseProof

Disclaimer:

Copyright 2013, All rights reserved.

No part of this publication may be reproduced, transmitted, transcribed, stored in a retrieval system, or translated into any language, in any form, by any means, without the written permission of the author. Understand that the information contained in this book is an opinion, and should be used for personal entertainment purposes only. You are responsible for your own behavior, and this book is not to be considered medical, legal, or personal advice. Nor is this book to be understood as putting forth any cure for any type of acute or chronic psychological illness. The programs and information expressed within this book are not medical or psychological advice, but rather represent the author's opinions and are solely for informational and educational purposes.

Cover design by Erica Wernick @ http://ericawernick.com

Table Of Contents

Free Bonus

As a special thank you for checking out this book, you may download your free "Why You're Stuck Quickstart" guide with quick tips and summaries from content in this book. You'll also get VIP updates on future book launches, discounts, and success tips.

Get it at: **http://derekdoepker.com/quickstart**

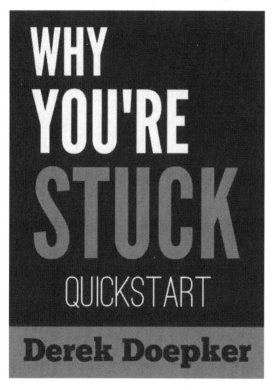

Introduction:

Do you want to know…

- How to tap into your inner strength to experience more motivation, happiness, and fulfillment on demand – regardless of what's happening in your life?
- How to get what you want even if you're stressed out, busy, or have a million excuses?
- What the most common fear is that holds people back, and why you'll never overcome it until you understand this one simple thing?
- Why it's impossible to remove a bad habit and what you must do instead?
- Why a force stronger than willpower may be your missing link to getting yourself out of any rut?

If you're feeling stuck, be it in your health, business, relationships, or overall happiness, you're in the right place. Maybe the day to day grind has gotten to you and you're looking to get something more out of life. Or maybe you know exactly what you want but don't know how to get it. Or perhaps you feel you lack the motivation or belief in yourself to make it happen.

This book will help you solve all these problems and much more. In addition to the benefits listed above, this book will also explain:

- What you can do when you have *no idea* what to do and don't know where to begin.
- Why much of the great advice you've heard, especially from self-help gurus, may be the very thing that's *keeping* you stuck.
- Why looking to find your life's purpose is almost always going to backfire on you.
- Why the truth gets you stuck more often than lies, and what the "real" truth is when it comes to you being incredibly motivated and successful.
- How being *selfish* can be the best thing for you and for the rest of the world.

- Why being stuck may be exactly what you *need* to make your next breakthrough.

The good news is, what you're about to learn will help you get out of whatever rut you're in regardless of your unique circumstances. Broke? Doesn't matter. Crazy people in your life? No problem. 300 pounds overweight? No big deal. No time to get things done? Makes no difference.

While each challenge has its own set of solutions, the reason we get stuck in various ruts can be broken down into a relatively small set of common mental and real-world barriers we all experience from time to time. Once you understand what's *really* been holding you back and why these things show up, you'll have a map to craft the perfect escape plan from your problems.

But before I go any further, you may be wondering who I am and what makes me qualified to teach this stuff. While I'm currently a bestselling fitness and motivation author, I obviously didn't start out this way.

My journey began when I was 17 years old. I was eating fast food every single night, never exercised, was terribly unhealthy, and no one could have paid me to change. Then, I discovered a few insights which you'll learn later that allowed me to do a complete 180, and get myself in great shape. Later on I started helping others do the same by sharing a few strategies to reprogram their thinking.

It would be another nine years before I became a bestselling fitness and motivation author. However, in the meantime, I started studying everything I could about psychology, motivation, personal development, and more to get to the bottom of why we do what we do and how you can literally reprogram your brain for more creativity, drive, and success in any area of life.

Yet despite having my body in great shape, I still had other areas of my life in need of major improvement. At age 25, I moved to Los Angeles to pursue a career in music. I had two jobs and could still barely pay the bills. I had studied enough about success that I felt this "shouldn't" be happening, and yet for a couple of years I could barely make ends meet.

Rather than letting this stop me, I dove deeper into studying what is different in those who are living highly fulfilling and inspiring lives from "the rest of us." I found several more insights that allowed me, literally within a few weeks, to achieve financial freedom. A book I wrote became a #1 bestseller, I started a business helping authors, and I've been able to wake up each day doing exactly what I want to do with my life.

After realizing just how powerful these insights are to completely transform one's life, I made it my mission to share what I've learned with others. I've done my best to distill down the most important concepts I've learned on my own journey, in order to help you achieve similar breakthroughs in any area of your life – be they financial, emotional, physical, or spiritual.

While you will find many practical solutions in this book for getting unstuck, my goal is to give you the tools to find your *own* answers. Your challenges will be unique to you, and there's no way anyone else in this world, even a great coach, can always tell you what's best for *your* life. So figuring out the solution is your job. I want you to be empowered to choose what you believe is best for you.

This is not a be-all-end-all book giving specific insights into becoming financially free, fixing a broken relationship, getting in shape, or anything else that requires specialized knowledge. It's a book that helps shed light on why those problems may have occurred in the first place, and it helps you draw out your own answers to figure out the perfect solution that works with your circumstances and unique psychology.

While much of what you're about to discover has taken me years of research to uncover through study and real-world experimentation and now I'm giving you the most essential things you need to know to overcome any challenge. I will warn you though, the most proven and time tested things are the simplest. I'd even be willing to bet you know quite a bit of this already, but you may not have any idea just how powerful some of these things are when you apply them regularly. People sometimes jump from book to book looking for answers, but get distracted by fluff and hyped-up gimmicks, when often the simplest solution is to get focused and apply what you already know.

Realize that simple doesn't always mean easy. I can give a person a simple exercise program that will transform their body rapidly and without fail, but it may be incredibly challenging and difficult. If you're not willing to do the practices and act upon what you read in this book, then that's your choice. Realize, however, that you're making the choice to *stay* stuck if you don't do anything. You don't have to and shouldn't believe anything I say without trying it for yourself, but whether or not you apply what you read here and/or get help elsewhere, things will not change in your life until you make the choice to change things. So ask yourself, "what's my life going to be in a year, or five years from now if I don't start learning and applying this stuff?"

If you're ready to discover what's really been holding you back, and take the steps to break free, keep reading, and discover the three biggest things that enable you to do this. These 3 keys are the foundation for understanding both why you're stuck and knowing how to get free. When you understand how to apply these 3 keys, you'll be able to breakthrough any challenge or obstacle that's been holding you back time and time again, so that you never again have to be lost, wondering "what the hell do I do to get out of *this*?"

Chapter 1: The 3 Big Keys To Getting Yourself Unstuck

There are countless reasons for getting stuck. You may not know what to do. You may know what to do, but not know how to get yourself to do it because you feel scared or unmotivated. Maybe you feel like there's nothing you *can do* because your problems are someone or something else's fault.

I can say from personal experience that I've been stuck due to all of these reasons and more. But no matter the situation, I've found there's always a way out. It didn't matter how complicated or hopeless the situation was, doing one of three things would inevitably set me on a path to freedom from whatever my challenge was. These are what I call the "3 keys to freedom."

The 3 keys to freedom from being stuck are **awareness**, **appreciation**, and **action** (choice). In a moment, you'll discover how all three of these things work together to both identify what's really keeping you stuck and how to overcome it. Before getting to that however, let's take a look at each one of these keys by themselves in more detail.

Key 1: Awareness

If you fell down a hole, knocked yourself out, and woke up to find yourself surrounded by total darkness not remembering how you got there, what would be the first thing you need to know to escape? It would be the awareness that you're in a hole. And if you've ever felt trapped by obsessive thoughts you can't get rid of, lost and confused about what to do or where to turn, overcome by emotions like anxiety and stress, and at the mercy of unwanted habitual behaviors and circumstances, then you know what it's like to have fallen into one of these "holes."

The first obvious reason why awareness is important is that you have to be aware of what the real problem is in order to overcome it. But is it enough to just know that you're in a hole (stuck), and to know how to escape (get unstuck)? If you felt like your life were perfect, if you had a lot of money, were in great shape, and filled with happiness, living the life of your dreams, what good would it be to have all of that only to lose it a few months or years down the road?

Unfortunately, this not only happens to many people, but it seems to be the norm – getting out of one hole only to fall into another. Coming from a health and fitness background, I can say that many people who lose a significant amount of weight often gain it all back again in a matter of months. While there are a variety of physiological and psychological reasons for this, the simplest explanation is that most people target the *symptoms* of their problems and not the root cause. This failure to get to the root of the problem also explains why some people who win the lottery end up broke years later, Also, some people get themselves out of one bad relationship, only to end up in another shortly afterwards.

What this means is that if you're not *aware* of what created your challenge in the first place, then even if you do break free, you'll just fall back into the same rut again down the road. It's not enough to have the awareness of *what* the problem is, you also need the awareness of *why* that problem developed in the first place so you can then figure out *how* to escape it and prevent it from happening again.

If you want to know what being blinded by a lack of awareness looks like, consider someone so engaged in texting on their phone that they walk headfirst into a pole. Before you laugh at them for being such an idiot, you may want to consider how many metaphorical poles you've walked into in your life because you weren't paying attention. We can all blind ourselves to what's right in front of us by ignoring the bills piling up, ignoring the gradual discontent of a partner in a relationship, or ignoring the feedback that people in our lives are telling us. Sooner or later, you will walk headfirst into a pole that just seemed to come out of nowhere.

Then, if you're like a friend of mine who often curses the inanimate object he bashes himself against, you may be tempted to blame the pole for "getting in your way." It's that damn pole's fault for getting right in the middle of where you were walking. This is a trick we play on ourselves because as long as something else got in *your way*, you don't have to change *your way*.

The pole in this example could be analogous to everything in our outer world that we can't control or change. This especially includes people who, no matter how much we wish they would think or act differently, are basically as set in their ways as the pole is set in the ground. And getting upset at them because they "should" be different is about as productive as getting upset with a pole you've run into that "should" have known better than to not be where you were walking. This isn't to say the answer is to avoid certain people all together as you'll learn about later, but rather to consciously be aware of and choose how you let them affect your life.

The only way to change what's in your way is to change your way.

Awareness has two parts – awareness that comes from within yourself and awareness that comes from outside yourself. The awareness that comes from within is like the light bulb that goes off in your head when you suddenly have an insight or see something in a new way. It comes from self-reflection – or the act of simply observing yourself. Awareness that comes from outside yourself is anything you see, hear, or experience that raises your awareness. If you've ever watched a documentary, read a book, or heard something said that raised your awareness on something and led to a near instantaneous change in your thinking and behavior, you know the power of gaining greater awareness from outside yourself.

One of the biggest shifts in my life was catalyzed by this type of increase in awareness. After years of living off of junk food, I made a radical change in my behavior to becoming a "health-nut" pretty much overnight. While there were multiple factors involved, the one thing I recall having the biggest impact was reading a book that explained the negative health effects of my dietary choices. It didn't just say eating trans-fats and excess sugar was "bad," it went into detail about what happens to the cells in the body, the hormonal changes that occur, and the exact process of pre-mature aging and disease. The book also revealed how particular supplements and health foods, which had no relevance to me before, could provide real world benefits like having more energy, looking better, and preventing sickness. It showed me in *explicit* detail the damage I was choosing to do to myself as well as what I was missing out on.

This type of awareness couldn't come from within. It required actively studying and researching information. After reading that book however, my awareness then shifted *inward*. I started to consider what my values were. Did I really want to be an unhealthy person for the rest of my life, or would I rather be a person that takes great care of themselves (and also look really frickin' amazing)? Once I had the internal awareness of how my unhealthy behavior wasn't in alignment with what I valued (or wanted to value), my actions very quickly changed. For the past 10 years, I've stuck with living a healthy lifestyle, which was all prompted by increasing my awareness.

While education is important for gaining awareness, the most important insights about how to fix your life will come from within yourself. This leads us to the first and most foundational practice to developing greater inner awareness – becoming both a participant and an *observer* of your life. This will help you uncover the various thoughts and feelings that are driving your behavior. Once you know these, you'll discover techniques later in this book for shifting how you think and feel about anything.

Key 2: Appreciation

Appreciation is recognizing how *everything*, even the most painful struggles and challenges, can serve to provide you greater freedom and fulfillment. This may seem difficult if not impossible to believe right now, but one of my main purposes in writing this book is to help you see how true this is. Whether or not something that's happening to you or has happened to you benefits you or harms you is a *choice* that's up to you to make. The thing that can set you free is also the thing that can keep you stuck, depending on your response to it. And while this might not make sense right now, you'll come to see later on in this book why this paradox is the reason why so many people get stuck.

Everything can either serve or enslave you depending upon your response to it.

Appreciation doesn't mean you have to like or enjoy something. Most of us don't like to experience physical pain. But imagine what would happen if you couldn't feel any pain. You'd get bruised up, burned, and you could potentially turn what would be minor injuries into life threatening ones by unknowingly aggravating them. You may even die of an easily curable sickness, all because you lacked pain to make you *aware* of something being wrong.

In this respect, you can *appreciate* how pain is serving you without actually liking it. Both physical and emotional pain/discomfort serve as great slaps in the face to make you *aware* of something so that you can take *action* to create a different experience. If you don't appreciate the service of pain, and therefore decide to numb yourself with drugs and/or distractions, you can miss the message the pain is trying to make you aware of, and fail to take a different course of action.

Distraction is morphine for the mind. Distraction is used to cut off your awareness to a problem, at the expense of cutting off your awareness to its solution.

Ignoring or resisting any type of pain is one of the most fundamental *root* causes of getting stuck. We've developed all kinds of defense mechanisms against feeling pain. Blaming, complaining, and justifying are all ways to reduce the pain that comes from being wrong, uncertain, or victimized. Criticizing and attacking others are ways to avoid the pain of our own insecurities. And as strange as it sounds, we may inflict pain on ourselves to distract ourselves from an even greater pain that we don't want to face.

As the pain is numbed, so is our awareness of what that pain is trying to show us about ourselves. Bedsores develop in paralyzed or numbed people when they stay in the same position too long. Normally someone would get uncomfortable and shift their position when a part of their body has had pressure put on it too long. However, when a person can't feel pain, they can develop huge gaping wounds unbeknownst to them all, because they didn't get the signal their body would have normally sent.

If you miss the message that the painful things in your life are trying to show you, you can develop emotional and psychological "bedsores." Things continue to slowly get worse and worse until eventually, something so big happens that you just can't ignore it anymore. For example, a relationship may slowly erode, until there's a huge fight and breakup due to all the pent-up resentment that was never addressed. Or a person suddenly realizes how badly addicted they are to alcohol, drugs, food, the internet, video games, or whatever they've been using to distract themselves from the painful things they didn't want to be made aware of.

One thing to note about appreciation is that it is not about only thinking happy thoughts (positive thinking) and feeling good all the time. Whenever you're going through a rough time, the last thing you usually want someone to tell you is to "stop worrying" and "cheer up!" That's because most of us feel that, even if others have our best interest at heart, they don't *appreciate* what we're going through.

Appreciation means embracing the fact that you won't only think happy thoughts, and sometimes you're going to feel miserable – *and that's OK*. This is because appreciation recognizes that negative thoughts are equally as valuable as positive thoughts. It's about appreciating both the positive and negative things, because only then can you have full awareness of the situation, and take action with all the facts. Sticking your head in the sand and pretending nothing can ever go wrong is failing to appreciate that sometimes bad things happen, and you'll need to be proactive about it. This overly optimistic approach to life can be just as destructive as an overly pessimistic approach.

Appreciation isn't gained by ignoring the negative and focusing on the positive; It's gained from accepting how both negative *and* positive are necessary for wholeness.

Appreciation also means compassion for yourself when you screw up. It even means appreciating yourself when you don't feel appreciation for what is happening – and yes I know that seems like an oxymoron. You can literally think, "I know I could be more appreciative, but I'm not, *and that's OK*." What you'll find is that when you stop beating yourself up over things, and appreciate wherever you're at in the moment by saying, "I feel XYZ – *and that's OK*," only then will you be able to break free from it. It's counter intuitive and paradoxical, but the best way to get over feeling bad is to allow yourself to feel bad – and yet be OK with that. This requires you to stop saying, "I should feel…" and instead just welcome and acknowledge how you do feel.

This means appreciation is more than just an intellectual appreciation of something. It's the actual ability to *welcome and allow* any particular thought or feeling without fighting it, and without becoming a slave to it. In this respect, you could say it's about *allowing* and *accepting* as much as it is gratitude.

Sometimes, so-called negative emotions like anger, fear, and jealousy are telling you a very important message that you need to pay attention to. If you resisted fear by ignoring it, you might not recognize genuine danger. If you went in the other direction, and became too attached to your fear, you might not escape genuine danger, because you'd be paralyzed by the fear. If instead you allowed fear to be there and actually thanked it for its service, you'd be able to recognize its message and still stay in control of the situation. Appreciation therefore turns your thoughts and feelings into things that serve you rather than things that dominate and control you.

It's only through a willingness to welcome whatever is happening to you rather than resisting it that you can get the message it has for you – and that message includes how to get yourself unstuck. In other words, within your problem is the answer of how to solve it. But you'll only discover this answer if you appreciate the problem, and are willing to embrace it.

Finally, appreciation is not about adopting the "at least it's not worse" mentality. This is really appreciating what a situation is *not* rather than appreciating what it *is*. This also explains why people who say "at least..." or "it could have been worse" in response to our struggles strike us as unappreciative of our situation. There's nothing wrong with recognizing your challenges could be worse, but it's still a distraction from facing what you're actually going through.

Key 3: Action (Choice)

The third key to freedom is to take conscious action. Taking action to change one's life is one of those stupid obvious things we all know we need to do, and yet somehow we manage to trick ourselves out of it by *imagining* a better life rather than doing the work of *creating* one. The good news is that by focusing on raising your awareness and appreciation, the best course of action tends to become both clearer and more desirable. This means if you've had a hard time struggling to get yourself motivated, you're going to learn how to get yourself to act even if you don't have a lot of willpower.

While much of this book will help guide you to make better choices, making any choice is the area that *you* have total responsibility for. It may be up to me as the author to help make you aware of certain things. I may even have a limited capacity to increase your appreciation for something by explaining its benefits. However, it is you who still has to make the choice to read this book, and act upon what you discover – even during the times you don't feel like it.

The purpose of this book above all else is to empower you to make your own best choices rather than tell you what you *should* do. This is in contrast to many books that are simply filled with a bunch of "do this, don't do that" types of advice that have a one-size-fits-all answer for everyone. Not only that, but it's always up to you to decide how you want to experience life. Part of the fun of life is getting to choose your own experience.

The biggest thing to understand with action is that you *always* have a choice in what you do – with perhaps only a very few exceptions. If someone puts a gun to your head and says they'll shoot you if you don't do something, you *still* have a choice – albeit not a very good one. You never *have to* do anything, but rather you can *choose to* do something because the alternative choice(s) are perceived as worse.

The reason why this distinction is important is that many people, when feeling stuck, think to themselves, "Well, I can't change anything, so I'm screwed. I'll just sit around and be miserable." Even if it's true you can't change something that is bothering you in the outside world, you can still always *choose* how you respond to it in your thoughts and feelings.

Remember: The ability to choose how you think and feel about your experience of life is the greatest freedom of all, because it is the only freedom that no one and nothing can ever take from you – even by physical force. This is true empowerment.

"The only disability in life is a bad attitude." - Matthew Jeffers

Chapter 2: 3 Keys Working Together

Even though I present these 3 keys in the order of awareness, appreciation, and action, they don't necessarily work in a step-by-step fashion. You can focus on any one of these areas and notice improvements. These three all work together and when one is increased, the others almost always increase with it.

To illustrate how these 3 keys work together, I'll give an example of my own from how I got the idea for this book. I had achieved some success and made major breakthroughs in the last few months, but instead of feeling stuck because of a lack of options, I actually felt stuck because I had so many options. Yes, I know this seems like a quality problem to have. But despite things being "OK" in my life, I still felt like I had some greater purpose to strive towards. It seemed like each day was going through the motions without any clear direction.

The first thing I did was look to increase my awareness, since that was what I seemed to be lacking. I spent time reflecting and meditating on what I could do, and still felt pulled in a number of different directions without anything inspiring me. I started taking some action by talking to friends, giving free coaching sessions, and looking around for answers as to what I could write a book about.

Talking to people gave me some more insight. This is because anytime you take action, you can gain more awareness. And with that awareness, I thought of more actions to take. I was using 2 of the 3 keys and while these things helped, I was still stuck.

I got more insight when I asked this question. "If I were coaching myself, what would I tell myself about how to get out of this rut?" This question really got me thinking about all the things I was doing (or not doing) that were keeping me stuck.

My real breakthrough came when I considered, "What if I'm stuck for a *reason,* and instead of it being a sign something is wrong, it's exactly as it *should be*?" In other words, I started seeing being stuck as something that was *serving* me rather than something that was holding me back. Then like a light bulb going off in my head, I had a sudden awareness of "What if I'm stuck and am working on getting myself unstuck, so that I can then turn around and share with others how I did it? What if this past month of being lost and confused was just to make me more aware of all the ways we get and keep ourselves stuck? What if within my problem was actually the solution?"

When I stopped fighting the problem and saw the problem not as a problem, but rather as the very thing I *needed*, this *appreciation* blew open the doors of awareness and gave me a choice of a new type of action I could take – to turn my challenge into an opportunity. In the act of breaking free of my own struggles, I would be given the insights into how I can help others do the same. But I could only come to this awareness and take a new course of action after *appreciating* and welcoming what I was going through.

Here's another example of how these 3 keys work with something like motivation. If most people were asked if they would run across a busy highway in exchange for $1, they'd say no. They're aware of the danger, don't appreciate the reward enough, and would make a choice based on what they felt served them the best – not risking death. But if a person needed to run across a busy highway to save the life of a loved one, they would be much more likely to do it.

What changed? The fear is still there, but now the appreciation that running across a busy highway isn't just a stupid thing to do – it's now a necessary and heroic opportunity to save a loved one. You might not actually *like* doing it, but you appreciate the necessity of it enough to act bravely because you're aware of the potential outcomes.

While it's easy to see this laid out in a simple scenario where you have all the facts, in real life you're not typically able to see all of these things. It would be more like being asked to run across a busy highway and being told "maybe it's for a good reason, maybe not." It's up to you to do the work to gain the awareness, appreciation, and take action to figure out whether things are or aren't worth the effort. Real life decisions are much harder because you don't get all the facts and must work to discover them for yourself, which takes time and effort. So you must appreciate that nothing here is meant to be an overnight fix - although that can happen too.

While not everything in this book will be spelled out as to how it relates to the 3 keys, realize that everything in this book is meant to, directly or indirectly, increase your awareness and appreciation so you can decide for yourself what choice is best for you. But even if you don't find your particular challenge directly mentioned, with these 3 keys, you now have a pathway to freedom from anything keeping you stuck.

Chapter 3: Developing The 3 Keys

Awareness Practice 1: Participant/Observer Awareness

The goal of awareness (or mindfulness) is to go throughout your day simply observing your thoughts and feelings as they occur *without judgment*. You become both a participant and curious observer of your life. By practicing mindful awareness, you can start to notice your habitual thoughts, feelings, and underlying beliefs behind every action (or inaction) you take. In doing so, you'll find many of the things that are keeping you stuck will become blatantly obvious.

Although it's a simple concept, it's not always easy. If you've ever found yourself doing something compulsively such as eating a bunch of chips while watching TV, or responding to a server's suggestion to enjoy your meal with a "you too," this a symptom of how we can be mentally absent minded by running on auto-pilot. I would argue that the majority of people most of time are *not* in a state of mindful awareness. This trance-like, autopilot state seems to be the default we fall into, and it takes *conscious*, focused effort to break free from it.

The first time I heard about this mindfulness practice, I didn't think much of it. Aren't I already aware of what's going on inside of me? I am someone that's often thinking a lot and very introspective. It turns out I was missing the boat. Most of the time that I thought I was being present and mindful, I was just operating on habitual patterns.

A simple example from my life of going from an unaware to aware state occurred after I logged into Facebook for what might have been the 17th time in a ten minute time frame. It was a distinct moment where I thought, "Why am I looking at Facebook again?" With further observation, I noticed how I was randomly jumping from website to website to kill time. At this point, I was aware of my behavior. However, I still needed to dig deeper, by being a *curious* observer, to figure out what was actually motivating that behavior. Was I doing this merely because I was bored? That might be a simple explanation, but then curiosity kicks in and asks, "Why would I be bored?" I certainly have plenty of things I could be doing; even entertaining things. The more I looked at my behavior and feelings, the more I found my actions were a result of wanting to distract myself from something. Naturally I wondered, "What is it that I don't want to face that is leading me to distract myself?" The further I went down the rabbit hole, the more I realized that logging into Facebook, checking emails, and wasting time on YouTube was a symptom *not* of boredom, but a way to take my mind off of the fact that I didn't feel like I really knew what I wanted to be doing with my life in that moment. I was feeling lost and confused about what direction to take, and this was so overwhelming that I was engaging in mindless behavior so that I wouldn't have to face such overwhelming feelings.

Had I not practiced any sort of mindfulness, I would have continued on distracting myself without giving it any second thought. Had I briefly questioned why I was doing that, *without being curious*, I may have thought "I guess I'm just bored" missing the incredible insight about myself waiting to be discovered by looking deeper. It's much easier to scoff a behavior off as stemming from boredom or feeling tired rather than seeing how it could be stemming from a need to distract oneself due to fear, overwhelm, or uncertainty – all of which are painful things to face. And most of the time what you don't want to face is *exactly* what you need to face to set yourself free.

This makes practicing mindful awareness deceptively more difficult than it first seems. Practicing awareness is not only challenging due to the fact that it requires mental effort, but it also takes a certain amount of strength to see the things you may have been purposely ignoring. You may instinctively want to tune out things and fall back into old patterns because it's far more comfortable. But like any other practice, the more you do it, the better you'll get.

Since it can be a bit scary to really look deep into yourself and face the things you've kept buried in your subconscious, the key to embracing this kind of inward focused mindful awareness is to remain in a state of total *non-judgment*. You must adopt the understanding that you are not those thoughts, feelings, fears, and other things you experience. If you were your thoughts and feelings, than who is it that is aware of those thoughts and feelings? Can thoughts be aware of themselves, or rather are you something greater than your thoughts? When you come to understand that you transcend all of this stuff going on inside of you, you're able to step into a place where you can simply observe what is happening without judgment and therefore without fear – or at least not overwhelming fear.

The kind of awareness we're talking about doesn't require you to dig up all of your past traumas to figure out how you got to where you are now. Instead, you can trust that whatever pops into your awareness at the present moment is whatever you need to be aware of the most. With this understanding that every moment is showing you exactly what you need to set yourself free, you can start to embrace the things that trigger a reaction in you such as fears, pet peeves, and unproductive habits as ways your mind is trying to make you aware of something.

Steps For Practicing Mindful Awareness

1. A "warm-up" exercise to get better at awareness is to just start to be aware of your right hand, or any part of your body for a couple of minutes. Put your mind into that body part and just notice all the feelings and sensations in that body part. Feel the temperature, the warmth of the blood flow, any air blowing across it, etc. Even though whatever body part you chose was always there, until you put your conscious attention into it, you probably didn't even really notice it. Similar to how hearing and listening are two different things, the difference being conscious effort, so is the difference between having thoughts and practicing mindfulness.

2. The next version of this is to start to apply this same level of conscious awareness to all of the thoughts and emotional feelings that come up inside of you whenever a strong emotional event takes place in your day to day life. Some questions to ask yourself include: What am I thinking? What

am I feeling? Why am I thinking/feeling this? If I did know why I was thinking/feeling this, why would it be? Simply let your natural state of curiosity take over you, and don't worry about whether or not you actually get an answer.

3. Then consider your various daily habits. This would be things like checking emails, driving, or eating food, etc. Pay particular attention to any bad habits you may be trying to break like smoking, screaming when upset, or keeping up with the Kardashians. Tell yourself ahead of time that you're going to make an effort to be consciously present and aware of everything that is happening inside you, especially during those times where you're usually operating on autopilot. There's a good chance when you first start that you won't really be totally mindful whenever you're doing something habitual. You may only catch yourself afterwards, and that's fine. Simply replay the experience in your mind and run through the questions such as "what am/was I thinking? How am/was I feeling?

4. As best as you can, begin to allow yourself to be mindfully aware and present throughout as much of the day as possible, through all activity and inactivity. This is the ultimate goal, and one you may work a lifetime towards. Just like you practice non-judgment when observing your thoughts and feelings, you must practice a non-judgmental and accepting attitude towards your likely *inability* to maintain this state constantly. Rather than "fighting" to remain mindful, simply bring yourself back to the present moment in a mindful state of awareness whenever you notice yourself having mentally checked out.

It's also important to remember that you're not trying to change anything about yourself, including your behavior, at this point. Just observe. Just notice. Just be curious. If someone wants to quit smoking, but also wants a cigarette, they can go ahead and have the cigarette. However, at the same time, they should try to notice what triggered their desire, how they felt, what they were doing right beforehand. As a pleasant bonus, you may find over time, that this practice of awareness *by itself* can be all it takes to get you to let go of unwanted habits and thoughts.

Awareness Practice 2: Daily Mindfulness Meditation

If you've ever felt like you've been stuck with unwanted thoughts, feelings, and overall anxiety, then I have some good news for you. While you may not be able to control every thought that enters your head, science has shown that regularly practicing meditation helps rewire the brain to give you more conscious control over how your thoughts affect you – even when you're not meditating. Scientists can even tell who meditates and who doesn't based on brain scans.

While I can't credit meditation for helping me overcome obsessive-compulsive tendencies (which I resolved before taking up meditation), I can say that meditation has had a profound effect on helping me remain in a peaceful, calm state all throughout the day without nearly as many obsessive thoughts.

I view meditation as rehab for the brain. Just like you can fix physical pain by strengthening muscles surrounding a joint, you can fix *psychological* and emotional pain by strengthening and altering certain connections in your brain. Studies have shown regular meditation creates physical changes in the brain that allow for a person to be more resilient to stress and less affected by anxiety. It also helps a person develop the ability to be more conscious of their behavior and less likely to simply react to something out of habit – essential for getting unstuck.

Steps For Practicing Mindful Meditation

Mindfulness meditation is simply the act of bringing your conscious awareness completely into the present moment. You'll observe your thoughts and feelings in a non-judgmental way, and refocus your attention to something like your breath. It's really no different than the previous mindfulness practice except you'll be sitting down and doing nothing while observing yourself.

The simplest meditation is a mindfulness meditation, like the one here:

1. Sit in a relaxed, upright position with your spine straight, and feet flat on the floor. Alternatively, if you're comfortable in a seated meditation position, you may do that.
2. Start to *focus* on your breath going in and out. Whenever your mind wonders, and it will, simply allow your focus to return to your breath going in and out. The actual act of refocusing your attention is part of the process training yourself to stay present. So it's OK if you find yourself having to refocus quite a bit.
3. If it helps you relax, you can mentally "scan" your body head to toe relaxing each muscle and body part.
4. Continue this for 5-15 minutes (start with just a few minutes daily), or as long as you're comfortable.
5. As you get more proficient at being able to focus only on your breath during meditation, you may begin to simply observe your thoughts coming and going. Rather than fight any thoughts because you find them distracting from the meditation, simply watch them pass through your awareness. It can help to think of yourself not as "me" or "my thoughts," but as an overall awareness of those things. You can ask yourself, "Am I these thoughts, or am I that which is aware of these thoughts?" As you do this, you'll find you more naturally let them go.

While the purpose of meditation isn't necessarily to try to stop all thoughts but rather observe them, if you really want to quiet your mind, you may mentally make the effort to watch for the next thought that is going to occur. Interestingly enough, the more you try to watch for the next thought to arise, the fewer thoughts seem to come, until your mind becomes quiet and still.

Even though meditation is an *active* process, don't worry about "screwing it up," and remember as long as you do it regularly with focused intent, even if your mind wonders a lot at first, you'll start to get better.

Appreciation Practice 1: Welcoming Your Experience

In conjunction with your daily awareness practice, ask yourself these questions when exploring any thoughts and feelings that come up. If your answer is no, remember you can be OK and appreciate that too.

- Can I welcome whatever I'm feeling right now? If not, can I be OK with not being OK?
- If I could appreciate what I'm feeling right now, would I? How would I appreciate this?
- Can I welcome and appreciate whatever I'm resisting?
- Can I welcome and appreciate whatever I'm attached to?
- Can I give myself love and acceptance even though I'm feeling and thinking this?

Appreciation Practice 2: Reframing Your Experience

Our language has a powerful effect on the way we perceive things. Just by changing the words you use to describe something, you will change your attitude around it. Notice whenever you use the word "problem" to describe something that's happening or has happened. Try substituting the word "problem" with the word situation, challenge, or opportunity.

You may also ask:

- Where is the opportunity in this challenge?
- Why is this challenge an opportunity?
- How can I make this challenge an opportunity?
- If there was an opportunity in this challenge, what would it look like?

Action/Choice Practice 1: Recognizing Your Choices

When going through your day practicing awareness, be aware of all the times you say the phrase "I have to" or "I must." You'll probably find yourself saying things like "I can't do that because I *have to* go to work. I *have to* visit my family. I *have to* watch the season finale of the Bachelorette."

Now ask yourself, is that really the case?

Really stop and consider if you *have to* do anything. I heard a friend say they couldn't do something because they had to take care of their son. While this seems like a valid excuse, I would rather say "*I choose* not to do that because taking care of my son is a bigger priority." This may seem like a small distinction in wording, but if you did nothing else but change your language to reflect that you *always* have a choice, you may be amazed to see how many problems start to fix themselves after noticing just how much control you have in your life.

If you find yourself using phrases that take away your ability to see a choice in the matter, consider these alternatives to your "have to's" and "musts."

- I won't
- It's not a priority / It's more important that I…
- I choose to (chose to)
- I choose not to (chose not to)

Action/Choice Practice 2: State Management

When it comes to taking action, it's very easy to get stuck in the trap of letting your emotions determine your behavior. You may feel tired, anxious, or uninspired, and simply want to kick back on the couch, instead of doing something like going to the gym or cleaning the house. It could be a more consistent pattern where each day you avoid taking care of something you know is falling apart because you feel too overwhelmed to even get started.

It's in these times that I've found comfort in knowing this – just as your emotions can influence your actions, *your actions can influence your emotions.* What that means is that, with a little willpower, you can take the necessary action to actually change your emotional state. Then once your emotional state is changed, taking more action becomes easier and easier. Sometimes the first step isn't to wait until you feel like it, but do it *until* you feel like it.

There have been many times where I was too tired to go work out. However, I found that if I told myself to just do three minutes of exercise and then stop if I wanted, I then could do more. I found that once I got going, my emotional state changed, and I would want to continue. And if I didn't feel better and wanted to stop after a few minutes, that was fine too. At least I did something, and didn't let myself become a slave to my emotions.

This also happens for me when I'm writing. The most resistance is in getting the process started. However, if I tell myself to only write 2 pages, and importantly give myself permission to have my writing be terrible, I find I get really into it and want to continue.

There were also times where the thing that kept me from writing would be anxiety. My head would be spinning, and I would make excuses about how terrible my writing was if when I wrote when I wasn't thinking clearly. So what I would do is give myself permission to relax for a minute and do nothing, then get up and do some physical movement like jumping up and down. Finally I would tell myself that I would just write a couple of pages, and if they suck it's ok. The point was that I was going to take some sort of action no matter what. Sure enough, I ended up getting over my anxious feelings to produce some quality work.

This kind of approach of doing just a small amount and allowing it to not be your best can be helpful when dealing with any sort of stress. Let yourself have a moment to feel the stress, anxiety, lethargy, or whatever else your feeling, then tell yourself you're going to *act* in the best way you can – even if it's just doing something really small. You may or may not feel better once you take action, but at least you didn't let your emotions run your life. The more you practice acting in spite of not being in the mood, the better you'll get.

You can act to change your emotional state with things like listening to music, chanting positive affirmations, and physical movement like exercise and dancing. While we all instinctively know this and may do it from time to time, it's very easy to fall into the trap of letting your emotions run your life. The key is to actually *remember* that you have control of your state. Throughout this book, you'll discover other techniques to change your emotional state, but it's still up to you to strive to take the right action, as best as you can, no matter how you feel.

Here are some questions you can ask when you don't feel like doing something:

- Can I allow myself to do just a little bit to try it, and then stop if I want?
- What can I do to change my emotional state?
- What action, no matter how small, do I feel like I can manage to do right now?

Chapter 4: What's The Real Problem?

What is it that's holding you back from what you want? Is it not having enough energy? Is it bad luck? Is it not having the right education? Is it the way you were born? Is it an unfortunate event or accident? Is it your family, friends, co-workers, neighbors, "the man," or anyone else? Do you have no idea, and *that's* why you feel stuck?

Whatever you think the problem is, you're probably wrong. How do I know this? Because if you really knew what your problem was, it wouldn't continue to be a problem unless you wanted it to be.

If your problem continues to be a problem, it's not the real problem.

To be fair, you may actually be spot on in your assessment of what's holding you back. I would argue that deep down inside, we have all the answers we need within us. What I'm really getting at is that we're typically very good at identifying and focusing on the surface-level issues that hold us back, but we don't really see where they stem from. In other words, we pick at the weeds but leave the roots intact. You must dig down deeper to see what the *real* root problem is behind your perceived problem. What this means is that **many of the things we consider to be problems are really just symptoms of a deeper root cause**.

If a person eats a food they're allergic to and breaks out in hives, they could take medicine to treat the hives. But they'd only be treating the symptom. Instead, they'd be better off getting to the root cause by avoiding the allergen. However, when a person only sees the hives and not what caused it, they may mistakenly attack the outward symptom rather than the deeper cause.

As a coach, my job has a lot less to do with solving people's problems, and a lot more to do with figuring out what their *real* problem is. Once the real problem is identified, the solution is almost always pretty simple and obvious to the person. In fact,

I'd be willing to bet that most of the advice you could ever read in any self-help or motivational book, including this one, is pretty much common sense. The real issue is that people have misdiagnosed their symptoms as root causes, and end up looking for the wrong treatment. No matter how great the treatment is, if it doesn't address your real issue, it's going to be a temporary fix at best.

I was talking with a woman who said she couldn't get herself motivated to write a book she had been wanting to write for some time. She said her problem was that she didn't have the energy or willpower to write after working all day. Now since this had gone on for over a month without a single word being written, I knew that wasn't her real problem. There had to at least be a few times where she could have set aside a half hour to get some writing done. Knowing that her perceived problem wasn't really the problem, I asked how she felt when she thought about writing. She felt scared. After a little more prying, I discovered she had unanswered questions about the publishing process, and felt overwhelmed by the thought of actually getting the book out. She lacked support in terms of technical issues like book formatting. She also lacked emotional support because she didn't have anyone telling her, "Yes, you *can* do this!" This is a common issue for people who don't realize just how important outside support can be to overcoming one's challenges.

So on one level, she wasn't wrong in saying her problem was a lack of motivation. If I had attacked the problem based on what she thought the core issue was, namely a lack of energy and drive, the advice I would have given her would have only had short-term results at best. I could have said to schedule some time each day; to get writing done in the morning, drink some coffee for energy, work on the weekends, create some accountability by paying someone money if you don't get a chapter written each week, or any other tips that *may* have helped if her problem was what she really thought it was.

Luckily, I understood what I'm sharing with you now. The problem is almost never what it first appears to be outwardly.

Real problems cease to be problems when you shine the light of awareness on them – at which point they become *choices*. After getting to what her real problem was, I offered some guidance on potential solutions. While this did require some technical knowledge of what she needed to do, I'd be willing to bet if she had properly identified the problem in the first place, she would have been able to seek out the resources she needed to get answers.

Remember that everything in your life can either enslave or serve you depending on how *you* respond to it. This means that no matter how much it seems like something external to you is the problem, and therefore beyond your ability to control, the only real problem is your inability to handle whatever you're dealing with.

If you can fix something, it's not a problem. If you can't fix something, it's not worth *making* it a problem.

Consider these questions:

- Is it the things that stress you out that's the problem, or is it your inability to manage stress?
- Is it lack of time that's the problem, or is it how you prioritize things in your life?
- Is it lack of resources (including money) that's the problem, or is it your lack of resourcefulness? *Credit to Tony Robbins for this.*
- Is it people's criticisms and harsh words that's the problem, or is it you taking those things to heart?
- Is it others not giving you love that's the problem, or is it you not giving yourself love?
- Is it things in your life making you unhappy that's the problem, or is it your choice to hold onto unhappy thoughts and refuse to let yourself be happy?

Before going any further, I want to say that even though I'm advocating looking at your response to things as a root cause of what's holding you back, I'm **not** saying *you* are the problem yourself. That's because, from the perspective of appreciation, there really is no problem – only challenges and opportunities. So even if you don't always respond to things the way you feel you "should," remember that even your mistakes contain within them the opportunity for growth. This requires separating your self-worth from your thoughts, feelings, and actions which come from you, *but are not you.*

I'm also not lifting responsibility from others to do their part – especially in relationships. It's certainty possible you could be dealing with people and circumstances that have created unnecessary challenges in your life at no fault of your own. You may want to ask yourself, "Do I want to let other people or life's circumstances have control over my happiness?" The only way other people or things can take your power to be happy and fulfilled away is if you give your power to them. This may be a hard pill to swallow, but when you appreciate this, you'll realize feeling happiness and fulfillment is within your control.

It could be said the ultimate root cause of any issue you'll ever have is the inability to handle whatever comes your way. T. Harv Eker says you must become bigger than your problem, and when this happens, it's no longer a problem. This means, rather than trying to avoid any and all challenges or obstacles (which is never going to happen), you must develop yourself be able to handle any challenges.

But the typical response is to want to avoid challenges and painful experiences. We see challenges, including things like feeling stuck and not having answers, as a sign something is wrong. What if it's a sign something is right? What if you being stuck and overcoming it is exactly the experience you need to grow to be able to handle any future challenges that come your way?

What if your problem isn't a problem, but the exact experience you need to make your next breakthrough?

An analogy to this is an Olympic athlete training to overcome their competition. Their competition could be considered the problem in as much as it's the competition that will keep them from winning the gold. What if the competition decides not to show up? What victory is there in winning a medal if you don't have any real challenge to overcome? If all you want is a gold medal, then you may wish to avoid competition all together – but it will be an empty and unfulfilling victory.

Growth, as you'll discover shortly, is an actual human *need*. You will not be truly fulfilled if you're not growing, and you will not grow if you don't have challenges to overcome.

The mindset adopted by champions is *not* to avoid or eliminate their problems, but to embrace their problems as exactly what they *need* to bring themselves to a higher level of development. The champion doesn't see their challenges or opponents as problems in the first place. How can something be a problem if it's there to help you grow? Doesn't this make it a blessing rather than a curse?

The answer to whether something is a blessing or a curse is dependent on your response to it. If you resist the problem (and you resist the problem by labeling it a "problem" in the first place), then it will always be seen as something trying to keep you down. When you believe something has the power to limit you and keep you down, then that's exactly what it will do.

However, if you see and even *welcome* the struggles, challenges, and obstacles you have, not as problems, but as a means by which you develop an unshakeable *inner* strength and peace that can't be taken from you, then those challenges become your greatest allies. Just as your muscles require resistance to be strengthened, your inner strength must be developed by having it tested. Courage isn't developed by *eliminating* fear, it's developed by *overcoming* it. Courage *requires* fear in the same way other virtues require their corresponding "shadow" vices. Whether you like it or not, while you're on this Earth, you don't have much choice but to accept that you'll face challenges that you can either face and overcome, or be destroyed by.

If you choose to see something as a problem, it *will be* a problem. If you choose to see something as an opportunity, it *will be* an opportunity.

Your experience of life results from your perception, and you can always choose your perception. Therefore, you can always choose your experience of life.

No matter what life throws your way, no matter how much your free will and sovereignty are stripped, you can still choose your internal response to anything. The only person who can enslave you in your inner world is yourself.

The ability to choose your response to what life throws your way isn't meant to make light of people who have "real problems" like having a family to feed, dealing with death of a loved one, fighting for survival. There are many conditions that aren't merely "in your head," aren't your fault, are unavoidable, and have very real consequences for wrong decisions. Realize it's this understanding that enables you to control your perception and will truly empower you, *especially* under the worst of situations.

This is what Viktor Frankl discovered when he spent three years in suffering some of the worst conditions on Earth -- in concentration camps during the Holocaust.

"When we are no longer able to change a situation, we are challenged to change ourselves." – Viktor Frankl

The challenges you face are real, as is the pain. There's no debating that. You can't wish for these things to go away. Any distractions like alcohol, drugs, reality TV, video games, celebrity gossip, Facebook, and funny YouTube cat videos, will be short-lived. What I am pointing out here is that no matter what happens to you in your outer world, you have the ability to choose how you respond to it in your inner world. When you consider that your experience of reality is really just your perception, you'll understand the truth of this statement: **The fate of *your* world rests in *your* hands.**

Now that you're aware of and appreciate the fact that the only real challenge you have to face is mastering your response to your circumstances, you're ready to discover why you think and feel like you do about everything in your life. Without understanding what motivates you, you'll find actually changing your attitude and beliefs to be extremely challenging. That's because everything you *currently* think, feel and do, no matter how much it's keeping you stuck, still benefits you in some way on an emotional level. Once you understand the six human needs you're going to learn about in the next chapter, you'll know exactly what drives you, be able to explore new ways of feeling fulfilled, and finally drop old unhealthy habits in favor of better habits *without* feeling deprived or constantly having to use your willpower.

Chapter 5: Why People Do What They Do (And Don't Do)

The idea that you need to "get motivated" or that you lack motivation is one of the biggest myths you'll ever tell yourself. You don't need to *get* motivated because you already *are* motivated. If a person can't get themselves up off the couch to clean the garage, it's not because they're "unmotivated." It's because they're *more motivated* to keep up with the Kardashians than clean. Even if someone consciously says they'd rather clean things up than sit around and watch TV, but don't because they lack the energy or drive, the important thing to understand is that you're acting on what you subconsciously believe will fulfill you and not what you consciously think you want.

Learning the six things that motivate you will help you determine *what* you really want, *why* you want it, and even open up new possibilities for how you can achieve happiness and fulfillment right now. Once I understood how motivation and fulfillment really worked, not only was I able to get myself to do just about anything I set my mind to, but I actually enjoyed the process rather than having to force myself into action through willpower.

The foundation of much of this book comes from understanding the six human needs that drive all of your behavior and using them to your advantage. Once you understand these six needs, you'll have a better understanding of why you do what you do, why some things aren't making you happy (and yet you may continue to do them), and how you can accurately identify something else that will make you feel more fulfilled.

Motivation is typically reduced to the simplistic idea that we want to gain pleasure and avoid pain, i.e., the carrot and the stick. It's helpful to know that pain is roughly three times as strong as motivator as pleasure. I would also argue for the inclusion of a third motivator – love.

While this pain/pleasure framework can be useful, it begs the question, "What causes *psychological* pain or pleasure?" Thanks to the work of Tony Robbins and Cloé Madanes in the field of Human Needs Psychology, we can see human motivation narrowed down to a set of six human needs.

These six human needs are:

1. Certainty (safety, comfort)
2. Uncertainty (excitement, variety)
3. Love (connection)
4. Significance
5. Growth
6. Contribution

To elaborate on why it's hard for a person to get themselves to give something up, such as watching TV in exchange for something else like working out, it's because they feel the old behavior meets their six needs to a greater extent than the new behavior. In other words, they'd feel a loss of pleasure and/or an increase of pain by sacrificing what they're used to. This is especially true if the person associates the new behavior with something painful, as is often the case when thinking about exercise.

No matter how much you may *say* or think you want something, if you don't feel motivated enough to get it, that means on some level your current behavior or circumstance is associated with meeting these six needs more than the new behavior or circumstance. And the same is true for getting motivated to give something up. If you have a hard time letting go of an old bad habit, it's because it is helping you meet one or more of these six needs.

Even though there are only six human needs that we all have in common, the way we prioritize and meet these needs are endless. This explains how we can all be *fundamentally* the same, and yet simultaneously outwardly unique. Some people may gain certainty by developing skill sets, others may gain certainty by blaming others and making themselves "right" all the time, and still others may gain certainty by following routines, like going to their favorite cafe each day. In other words, there are healthy, unhealthy, and neutral ways to meet these needs. And any action, even beneficial ones, when taken to an extreme can become unhealthy.

Let's take a closer look at each of these needs and how they may play out in a person's life.

Certainty

The need for certainty can be seen in our desire to have comfort, security, and stability. If you are familiar with Maslow's Hierarchy of Needs, the most fundamental need to be met is our need for survival. This would include our need for food, water, and shelter as well as the ability to secure these things over the long-term with resources/money, employment, health, and property. It's our desire for certainty that typically prompts us to get these things, and it's also our desire for certainty that drives us to avoid risk by creating a *fear* of losing these things.

Desire for certainty doesn't just apply to our survival needs however. Things like following routines, seeking advice, and carefully considering options before making any choices are all ways a person can meet their need for certainty. One of the biggest ways people get certainty is by blaming self or others. The lack of certainty of not knowing who or what's at fault for a problem is why we typically feel compelled to want to place blame somewhere, anywhere,) when something goes wrong.

When the need for certainty is taken to an extreme, it may lead a person to types of excessive behavior, such as obsessive working, dieting, or exercising – which in themselves are great in moderation. A person can become extremely rigid and inflexible in their behavior. Those with obsessive-compulsive disorder often have a strong impulse for gaining certainty from their routines. One may even attempt to manipulate and control others to gain certainty. When a person lacks healthy ways to obtain their need for certainty, like having a steady job to secure income, they may resort to things like theft.

One of the more common reasons people get stuck is they over-prioritize certainty, or at least over-prioritize gaining certainty through *external* means like acquiring resources as opposed to relying on *inner* confidence. Common situations in which people find themselves stuck, like being overwhelmed, being unable to take risks due to fear of failure, or being unable to act because of not having all the right answers, are all driven by a need for certainty. "Better the devil you know than the devil you don't" directly speaks to our need for certainty, and living by this motto pretty much guarantees that you will stay in your comfort zone.

Uncertainty/Variety

The need for uncertainty can be seen in our desire for excitement, novelty, variety, and entertainment. While we all want to have a basic level of certainty in order to feel safe and secure, if things were *too* certain then we'd quickly feel bored.

A good example of a person wanting a mix of both certainty and uncertainty would be someone reading reviews for a movie before seeing it - *without* wanting to know the spoilers. The act of reading a review is to gain *certainty* that the movie will good, but avoiding any spoilers helps preserve a sense of *uncertainty* which adds to the excitement and surprise. Wanting two opposite things is paradoxical, but in a later chapter we'll discuss the importance of paradoxes, and how to work with them.

A person who is considered "free spirited" may have a stronger desire for uncertainty and excitement when compared to someone who may be considered more grounded and careful. If a person gets bored very easily, they may have higher uncertainty needs. Most forms of entertainment and recreation meet a person's needs for uncertainty.

Taken to an extreme, those who want a lot of uncertainty may engage in overly risky behavior for the sake of seeking thrills. They may also subconsciously stir up drama and chaos with their strong desire for excitement. So if you know any overly dramatic people and wonder why they would purposely create drama, this can be one motivating factor.

Love/Connection

It should come as no surprise that we all want to feel love and connection. This desire explains behaviors done out of a desire to fit in with others. From a survival standpoint, this makes a lot of sense. We couldn't survive and thrive without the assistance of one's tribe. Anything that makes us feel like an outcast will violate our desire for love and connection.

Our desire for relationships and communication reflect this need. Typical ways a person may meet this need would be caring for others, socializing, and acts of giving.

Take to an extreme, a person may sacrifice their own morals, beliefs, and standards in order to fit in. On a more emotional level, someone can become overly concerned with other's opinions of him. One may enter into unhealthy and even abusive relationships in order to feel a sense of connection. At a lesser extreme, a person may over-extend himself in an effort to do everything they can for others, while putting their own needs on the back burner. In other words, he'll sacrifice *self-love* in order to feel connection and love from someone else.

While love and connection is an important need, it's clear that like anything else, prioritizing connection in an *unbalanced* way will lead to unhealthy behaviors and feeling unfulfilled. If a person fears losing his connection with someone so much that he is unwilling to be vulnerable, then what happens is the exact opposite – he's *unable* to really connect and love on a deeper level. When we meet our needs with a fear and scarcity-based mindset, we actually close ourselves off from experiencing these things to their fullest extent.

"You can only love, and be loved, as much as you're willing to have your heart broken." – Dr. Brene Brown

Significance

Just like certainty and uncertainty appear to be opposites, but co-exist to create a balanced whole, significance is on the other end of the spectrum from love – though they're not exclusive from each other. To understand this, consider that our desire for connection makes us want to *fit in*, but our desire for significance makes us want to *stand apart*. In other words, we all want to feel special and unique. In general, women tend to more strongly favor love and connection over significance, whereas men typically have a stronger bias towards significance over love and connection.

The more you try to fit in, the less you appreciate how we're all unique. The more you try to stand apart, the less you appreciate how we're all the same.

A person may meet their significance needs by mastering a skill, putting themselves in the spotlight, or engaging in competition. In general, anything that makes a person feel unique and special is meeting their significance needs. Significance is also important in that it keeps a person from getting walked over from other people like a door mat. When a person ignores their need for significance, they may let themselves become bullied and abused by others.

Significance taken to the extreme can lead to controlling, manipulative, abusive, and egotistical behavior. A significance-driven person may trample on anyone and everyone else to reach the top. One may sacrifice his connection to others in order to satisfy his own ego - and yet never be satisfied, because this need for significance has been taken in isolation of other needs like contribution and connection. One may adopt the attitude that it's better to be feared and respected than loved. The behaviors associated with dictators and rulers who abuse their power are often driven by significance.

It's also possible that when a person feels they *can't* get love, they'll go for significance instead. This explains why a person or group who knows of no way to feel love may do things to provoke a reaction out of people in order to feel significant – which explains hate groups. They know if they send hate, they'll receive hate, and therefore gain a level of significance.

Why does anyone do this if people normally don't like to feel hated? Because it's at least better to be hated than ignored from a human needs standpoint. If someone is ignored, they can't meet their love/connection needs **or** their significance needs.

We can see that when a person emphasizes their need for connection at the expense of significance, they'll often end up destroying themselves, or allowing themselves to be destroyed by others. The danger in significance over-emphasis is that it tends to lead to behaviors that are *outwardly* destructive to others (and in the end oneself). While it wouldn't be totally accurate to say one need is better or worse than another, too much desire for significance can easily become the most devastating imbalance for its ability to cause a person to harm others physically and/or emotionally.

Growth

Growth and contribution are considered the spiritual needs. Another way of looking at them is that they're necessary for one to feel completely fulfilled. A person who has met all their other needs can go along just fine without feeling like anything is majorly wrong, but a part of them will feel like something is missing. They'll be left wondering, "Is this all there is to life?"

In Maslow's hierarchy of needs, these would be associated with self-actualization, which typically occurs after one has met their more primal needs of security, connection, and esteem. However, that's not to say a person may not feel a strong desire to grow and contribute even if they're lacking in other areas.

The need for growth explains one's desire to reach his fullest potential, learn for its own sake, and develop skills without any tangible benefit, like making more money. This need is also necessary to push yourself out of your comfort zone. It's part of what drives athletes, entrepreneurs, and other high performers to purposely take risks and experience pain in order to come out wiser, stronger, and overall better for the experience. Your desire for growth is what you use to pick yourself up after you have any type of setback.

The ways a person may meet this need are by reading books, developing a skill, and purposing challenging themselves. The more one has a need for growth, the more comfortable they are with failures and mistakes, *if* they recognize them as learning opportunities. Challenges in life are actually necessary in order to fulfill your need for growth. This is why, among other reasons, I recommend framing your problems as challenges to be overcome. This will tap into your innate desire to grow as a person. Without problems to solve or resistance to overcome, you'd feel stagnate, uninspired, and ultimately unfulfilled.

"Challenges are to the mind what exercise is to the muscles, they toughen and make us strong." Norman Vincent Peale

When a person has ignored their need for growth, or let other needs supersede it, they may find themselves unable to face risks, go through uncertainty, or continue forward after setbacks. This need is absolutely critical to embrace if you wish to push yourself beyond your current limits that are keeping you stuck.

Contribution

Contribution is our need to feel like we make a difference in the world and have a purpose. Many people, when facing death or after having a near-death experience, have said that when looking back on their lives, they forget about what they've personally acquired and think more about what they've contributed to the world. When you're faced with death, you may wonder "Did my life make a difference?" And when you consider your own inevitable death in day-to-day life, you may ask, "Am I making a difference *right now*?"

Everything you gain for yourself dies with you. Everything you give to others lives beyond you. The only lasting treasure is your impact.

Although contribution could be considered to be related to love and connection, acts done out of a desire to contribute typically don't require the recipient to acknowledge or be aware of the giver. A person giving in order to *receive* someone's approval would be done out of a desire for connection, but a person giving without expectation of getting anything in return is fulfilling their need for contribution. For instance, when a person makes an anonymous donation, it's usually out of a desire to contribute.

"I don't know what your destiny will be, but one thing I do know: The ones among you who will be really happy are those that have sought and found how to serve." – Albert Schweitzer

In my own life, the acts done out of a desire to contribute are things that I feel will impact people I'll never even meet. They're what I feel will have an impact even after I've left the earth. You could say contribution is more motivated by giving *unconditional* love with no strings attached rather than love/connection which can take on a more give and take dynamic. That being said, both of these needs (and all of the needs) work together. So a person more driven by love/connection may also find themselves more motivated to contribute – just not always.

I've noticed that the more a person is stuck in the day-to-day grind, the less likely they are to be focused on growth and contribution, and the more likely they are to be focused on their other four needs. Unfortunately, this is one of the biggest ways people *stay* stuck, because it's *through* growth and contribution that one will discover how to break free of the day-to-day grind. The only way to break free is to take a leap of faith and start investing in both yourself and others beyond your short-term desires and more focused on a long-term gain – without a guarantee of outward success.

Six Needs Working Together

It's important to understand that we all want each of these six needs, but the degree to which we prioritize some needs over others is unique to each of us. Also, the order in which we prioritize our needs can change over time – even over the course of a single day.

For instance, a person may follow a relatively set routine each day to meet their certainty needs. Then every few months, they may get the urge to take a vacation to meet their uncertainty/variety needs. Another person may tend to follow a set routine during the first half of their day, and then in the evenings do something fun for their variety needs. Still other people may choose jobs and activities that will meet both their certainty and variety needs. There are endless ways in which these needs cycle back and forth in an attempt to balance each other out giving rise to all our different personalities and preferences.

Oftentimes, the things we enjoy doing the most are things that meet most if not all of these needs simultaneously. For myself, writing books meets all of these needs to a high degree. I feel certainty because writing and publishing is something I'm used to doing. I also feel uncertainty/excitement because every book is different. I don't know where the creative process is going to take me, and I have no idea what people's reactions are going to be. I feel connection to others because sharing my message helps me form relationships with my readers. I feel significance because being an author brings me attention, and any success I achieve gives me validation. I experience growth because each book I write forces me to learn new things and challenges me. Finally, I feel contribution because I get to potentially change other people's lives, and leave something behind that can continue to have an impact even if I'm no longer alive.

If you consider what you're most passionate about, you'll likely see that it meets all or most of the six needs. Even if someone would hate doing something you love doing, while you'd both share the same basic six needs, the difference would be that you associate the behavior with meeting these needs, and they don't. This just goes to show you that whether or not an activity or even a way of thinking meets your needs is largely due to your subjective perception.

How Do Our Needs Get Us Stuck?

You can see by now that if you have a behavior that you don't like (including thinking and feeling a certain way), but still continue to do, it's A) because it's meeting at least one *or more* of your needs and B) because you haven't found a better alternative to satisfy the need(s).

Imagine the behaviors you use to meet your need as vehicles that get you to the destination of more certainty, more love, more significance. Trying to change what you do without having a better alternative (adopting a healthier behavior or mindset) is like ditching your worn out vehicle in the middle of the desert, and being stranded with no other means of travel. What happens here is you may just hop into the car of any passerby willing to give you a ride, even though that person could be dangerous.

In much the same way, we may abandon an old behavior when we recognize it's not healthy, but if we don't have a better alternative, we could latch onto whatever else comes our way that meets the same needs. A classic example is a smoker who gives up smoking only to turn to overeating.

A reason people get stuck in unhealthy patterns of behavior is because they haven't found any alternative ways to meet some need(s). If a person only has one vehicle to meet their need of love, and that's by getting people to feel sorry for them, then they will have *no other choice* but to play the role of a victim looking for sympathy. Telling them to "suck it up" and "deal with it," even if they *want* to overcome their "woe with me" attitude, typically won't work because it would be asking them to give up on the only way they know how to feel love and connection.

This is why you must become aware of how you're meeting your needs with your beliefs and behaviors, discover which of these beliefs and behaviors you've adopted that are keeping you stuck, and finally which beliefs and behaviors can be adopted instead to get you unstuck.

It has been my observation that people who seek to fulfill their needs through *external* means, with the exclusion of contribution and growth, will almost always find themselves stuck in some way. For instance, if a person can only get their significance needs met by getting praise from others, then they have no control over whether or not they feel significant, since it's always in other people's hands. This also means as soon as they get criticized, because they're placed their value on the opinions of others, they get extremely upset. When meeting your needs is dependent on other people or circumstances over which you have no control, you're setting yourself up for an eventual emotional disaster when things don't go your way.

A much healthier approach is to find the certainty, variety, love, and significance that's available within *yourself* at all times, and let go of needing to get it from the outside world. While letting go of things like wanting to control people and gaining approval may take time and practice, it's worth noting that it's the only way to real lasting fulfillment. Much of this book, even if it isn't directly stated, is designed to help you cultivate an inner fulfillment of these needs, so that you no longer have to depend on people or circumstances to satisfy these needs. Another highly recommended resource for this is the Sedona Method.

Practice: Become Aware Of Your Vehicles

We all have a variety of "vehicles" or methods we use to meet our six needs – both in what we do and in how we think. Chances are, you have behaviors that are healthy, neutral, and potentially unhealthy that you've adopted to meet your six needs. Remember, even a healthy behavior can turn unhealthy in excess. So even if your actions and attitude aren't *inherently* bad, realize that anything can become destructive if it's out of balance with something else.

Explore the following questions:

- How am I meeting my need for certainty? Uncertainty? Love? Significance? Contribution? Growth?

- Are there certain needs I value more than others? You can take this test to help determine which needs you prioritize. http://robbinsmadanescoachtraining.com/six-human-needs-test/
- Is there a need(s) that I'm not fulfilling as much as I'd like?
- How can I find a good way to meet that need?
- What are the healthy or neutral ways I've chosen to meet my needs?
- Can I allow myself to do more of those healthy things?
- What are the unhealthy ways I've chosen to meet my needs? What vehicles are causing me or others pain?
- What better things can I do instead of these to meet those same needs?

Chapter 6: How To Find Your Next Step

You may at this point have identified a few things that are keeping you stuck, and understand why you do them. What if you don't know what else to do instead, or how to move forward? It's one thing to know how to get yourself motivated and avoid pitfalls, but it's another to see a clear path of where you want to go. Maybe you've even been making great progress, but suddenly are finding yourself feeling unfulfilled from things that used to make you happy, but just aren't doing it for you anymore.

Even the most successful people at times will be left wondering "what's next?" I myself am very clear on my desire to contribute and grow, but I can still struggle figuring out just how exactly I'm going to do that. Do I write a book? If so, what kind of book? Do I coach more people? What do I coach them on? Do I focus on my other talents and start a new business? Should I try to reach a different audience? What really is my life's purpose and how am I going to fulfill it?

For others, their situation could be far worse. All they know could have been stripped away from them. They're suddenly left without a job, relationship, or lifestyle they're used to. Maybe it's been a slow process of making compromise after compromise until one day a person wakes up and realizes just how many regrets they have. They may have no idea how to feel happy and fulfilled or even where to begin. Maybe they know what they want, but feel it's just not worth the time and energy to try to get it – or don't know how to get the time and energy that's necessary.

This uncertainty and confusion, *when resisted*, can be a powerful force that keeps people stuck due to overwhelm, hopelessness, apathy, or sheer lack of drive. However, uncertainty is not to be considered something inherently bad. Not always having a clear direction or answers on what to do *doesn't* mean something is wrong. After all, you don't really want to invest a lot of time and energy into something that you later realize wasn't what you wanted all along. I'm sure you can remember a time when you've worked hard for something, only to feel empty after getting it. Even worse is the idea of putting time and energy into something that doesn't succeed at all. In this respect, feeling uncertain and stopping yourself from taking action can, at times, act as a safeguard from going down a potentially wrong path.

Going through periods of confusion and chaos are all a part of the process of discovery. This challenge only turns into a "problem" whenever you resist this confusion and don't know how to work through it. With this understanding, you can see that going through times of uncertainty is both normal and potentially beneficial if you respond to it correctly. The more you feel lost, confused, and uncertain, the more likely you'll be to stop what you're doing, and make the effort to reconsider what matters most to you.

The great benefit to being stuck is that it forces you to evaluate what's most important in your life at this very moment.

This means that even if you're not yet aware of why you're stuck, just the fact that *something* is making you feel stuck, is enough of a signal to get you to check out this book and start exploring what's going on in your life. The awareness that you're stuck is a siren going off telling you that you need to do some exploration into your beliefs, values, and behavior.

From this place, can you see how you being stuck might actually be exactly what you need to move forward? Could being stuck not be the thing that's holding you back, but actually be the challenge that's going to help you make a major breakthrough? What if you had to get stuck in order to learn lessons that can only come from getting yourself unstuck?

So how do you break free from this state of uncertainty and gain enough perspective to figure out how to move forward? It's starts with understanding this – you'll rarely be aware of the bigger picture, but you can always find the next step *if* you're moving forward. This is similar to driving a car at night. The headlights will only illuminate the immediate area ahead of your car, and yet that is enough to get you to where you're going even if it's hundreds of miles away. Just like you can't see what's further the road until you get there, you might not be able to see what's weeks, months, or years down the road for you until you get there – but you always see just enough to keep moving forward to your destination.

You don't need all the answers, just the next step. You can drive all through the night only seeing what's right in front of you.

I've continually found myself getting stuck in wondering what my next project should be. As an author, it's taken the form of finishing one book and wondering what to write about next. With so many possible directions to go in, I've found myself completely overwhelmed and confused. So I've done what most people do in this situation I've distracted myself with useless activities to take my mind off the uncertainty, and just sort of hoped the answer would come to me in a flash of inspiration.

The reason I couldn't see my next step was because I wasn't *moving forward*. I had to take action on what I *did* know before I could gain greater perspective on what I *didn't* know. What this means is that at times, you have to find the smallest constructive action you can take – and that becomes your next step. For me, I've had to ask myself, "Even though I'm not ready to start my next book, what can I do to be moving forward?" This meant reading books, talking to people and picking their brains, and learning about new subjects. Once I started acting on these things, I got more and more clarity, until I finally discovered the answer.

Looking back, going through that period of not having answers wasn't really a problem at all. I *needed* to be confused in order to discover new resources and insights that are now included in this book. This means the problem was actually the solution – and the solution was within the problem. Recognizing this paradoxical dynamic is the heart of appreciation.

If I stayed stuck longer than I needed to, it was because I resisted the problem by distracting myself. I was waiting for inspiration to suddenly come to me before moving forward, instead of realizing that it's through moving forward that inspiration comes. The issue with waiting for sudden flashes of inspiration to give you answers is that's not how great ideas really come about. Yes, it may seem like sometimes a great idea just pops into your head, fully formed from out of nowhere, while you're going on about your day-to-day business. Great ideas are actually a product of many smaller, seemingly insignificant insights that eventually combine together in your subconscious mind, and then pop up into the light of your awareness. You probably have many "seeds" of great ideas already planted in your head, but they just require a little more watering and nourishment before they sprout up into the light of your awareness as a fully formed concept.

Insight may come in a moment, but it results from an ongoing process.

Gaining Perspective Step 1: Set Your Focus

It's important to understand that you'll only get an "aha" moment if you've directed your subconscious mind to be on the lookout for the insight. In other words, you must give your mind the command (intention/focus) to look for answers in a particular area. This leads us to the first step in gaining perspective, setting your focus.

What you're aware of is significantly less than what comes through your five senses. Driving down the road, there's a good chance you don't remember all the license plates you see, signs you drive past, or types of cars on the road. The brain's Reticular Activating System is designed to filter out any information it considers useless. This means answers to all of your questions could be right in front of you, and you literally will not be aware of it unless you give your mind the command to allow that information to come through *unfiltered*.

When you tell your mind what to focus on, it oftentimes will start to go to work automatically to find answers even below your conscious awareness. As a musician, when I find myself spending days at a time composing and writing songs, I'll notice musical phrases and melodies come into my head while making lunch or exercising in the gym. Even though I'm not consciously trying to think of these things, I've set my subconscious focus so strongly to come up with these things that it happens automatically – even when I've stepped away from my instrument. The same thing happens with ideas for book content when I'm spending a lot of time writing. I will rarely get musical ideas **and** book ideas during the same periods of time, because I'm usually only *focused* on one thing or another during a particular day. As powerful as the mind is, it will typically respond to what you consciously tell it is *most important* to you at the moment.

So how do you tell your mind what to focus on?

While sheer intent will work, the practical answer is by *asking questions* – specifically the right kind of questions. And whether you realize it or not, you're already doing this quite a bit.

If you're asking yourself disempowering questions like "What's wrong with me?" "Why can't I figure this out?" "Why is everything so hard?" then those are the things your mind will focus on. Asking questions that imply you're going to stay stuck will guarantee you'll stay stuck. They're the nail in the coffin.

Something as simple as asking "How will I find the answer?" "Why am I getting even more clear?" or "Why are things getting easier and easier?" will all direct your mind to positive outcomes and solutions.

Another thing to keep in mind is that the very same question can be empowering *or* disempowering depending on your intent and emotional state. I see this all the time when people ask things like "Why should I be the one to do this?" "What's the point?" "What can I possibly do?" Whenever people ask these questions in exasperation throwing their hands up in the air, they take on a hopeless and disempowering sort of quality.

When you ask the same question slamming your fists down on the table and getting serious, it becomes very powerful. "Why SHOULD I be the one to do this? Because dammit, I'm smart enough, strong enough, and ready to kick some ass. No one else is going to do it for me, so I'm going to take fate into my own hands and create the outcome I want."

The questions you ask yourself in desperation, when made empowering by pumping up your emotional state and resolve, can be the *exact* question you need to discover how to break free of whatever is holding you back.

Start to notice the questions you ask yourself and identify them as either empowering, disempowering, or questions that *could be* empowering if you took them seriously.

Questions For Greater Clarity
1. What's my next step?

The significance of this question is that you only have to worry about your *next* step. If you find yourself tempted to start to thinking about what's 10 steps down the road, what you need to do a month from now, or anything else besides what's immediately relevant, then you need to remember you're only focusing on the very next thing. This requires making a leap of faith that more answers will come as you start to move forward, just like the next part of the road will be lit up when you're driving at night.

The biggest obstacle to moving forward seems to come when the mind projects, and starts to dump all sorts of unanswered questions and concerns on you in the present. *"What will happen if they say this? What if they do that? What if I screw something up? What if this thing goes wrong?"*

What you'll almost always find this does, is keeps you from taking any action because you're scared you're going to get overwhelmed down the road. This is an illusion. What's happening is that your mind is making you think you'll have to suddenly deal with all of these things at once, but in reality you'll only ever have to deal with your *next* step. Remember, even though you can't handle everything, you can handle anything - *one thing at a time.*

This does not negate the importance of planning ahead or being prepared. It does, however, require a healthy amount of being willing to "cross the bridge when you get there" type of mentality where you act without all the answers. It's the ability to find the balance between these two extremes. You'll learn more about how to do as you go through this book. Another way of looking at it is if your next step is planning, then plan. Remember that no amount of planning will give you as much perspective as doing – and it's through doing things that you'll be able get a better idea of how to plan.

2. If I DID know my next step, what would it be?

If your answer to question 1 is "I don't know," then ask yourself this question. The "if I did know" allows you to activate your imagination and the higher part of yourself that really does have all of the answers. The importance here isn't to worry about whether your answer is right or wrong, but rather to simply allow your mind to explore the possibilities. In other words, just frickin' come up with something instead of over-analyzing things.

"At the center of your being you have the answer; you know who you are, you know what you want and you know what you need to do." – Lao Tzu

Another way to get answers when you're not sure is to pretend you are yourself five years down the road as an older, wiser, and more knowledgeable version of you. I consider this to be a sort of self-guru type of approach where you literally pretend to be a guru who has the answers you're currently looking for.

You can also ask:
- "5 years into the future, after I have solved this, what would I go back in time and tell myself about this situation?"
- "If within my challenge was the solution, what might the solution be?"

- "If I were to tell someone else how to handle my situation, what would I say?"

3. What can I do right now to get even more perspective?

This question helps you remember that finding answers is a process. You might not know what you need to do tomorrow, but you can at least figure out something to do right now to get clarity. This could include things like reading a book, talking to a coach or friend, meditating, taking a walk, etc.

Variations on this question could include:
1. What can I do today to get answers?
2. Even if I don't know what to do, what might I *try* doing that *could* help?
3. What would fill me with joy, happiness, and fulfillment?
4. If there's something I could try, just to see what happens, what would it be?
5. How can I make a difference today regardless of whether it leads to anything else?

Gaining Perspective Step 2: "Act Then Analyze"

Once you have an idea that seems worth pursuing, it's time to make a choice to act on it. The key thing here is to remember that this type of action is meant to inspire more awareness and clarity, and it's less important that what you do is the "right" thing over the long haul – it's more about the exploration.

For instance, if a person is exploring a new career path, he may intern at a place temporarily just to try it and see if it feels right to him. If loves it, great. If not, he can always choose not to pursue that career. However, he would never know either way if he didn't at least give it a shot. Even if the person decides not to continue at the place where he interned, he may have learned more about himself and his skills, so that he now has a better idea of what he *does* want to do. That means the experience, instead of being a waste of time, was actually exactly what they needed to get the answers they were looking for. Remember that your level of awareness and appreciation will be limited by how much action you take.

There are two extremes of people when it comes to taking action. The first type of people are risk takers, who jump head first into things without thinking too much. By this point, you should know these people value uncertainty to a greater degree than certainty. The other type of people are cautious, conservative, and highly analytical people who will tend to take a long time to make decisions, and may go back and change their decision multiple times. These people value certainty more than uncertainty.

Each of these types has its pros and cons. Each can also get stuck. The risk-takers are great at getting things done, but they're also more likely to screw things up - majorly. They will usually either win big or lose big with their ability to make ambitious decisions without as much hesitation. They often get stuck having to pick up the pieces of their mistakes. The analytical types run the risk of accomplishing absolutely nothing due to inaction or slow action, but at least they can say they never made a major mistake. These people are more likely to get stuck overthinking everything, and not putting things into action.

As with all things, the solution comes when one can find the middle path. This means striking both a balance between taking *calculated* risks; risks that are neither reckless nor dependent on absolute guaranteed success.

Being an analytical person myself, I tend to find myself stuck in overthinking things to the point of paralysis by analysis. The simple phrase I say to myself to help me break through is "Act, *then* analyze." Since greater perspective typically comes *after* taking action, this makes action the *first* step. Then once I've done something, I can sit back and analyze my results and look to see what my next step is. When the back and forth cycle between these two things happens almost simultaneously, this is what we call a state of "flow."

I want to point out that "action" can include the act of brainstorming, and isn't necessarily limited to outward action. The reason why brainstorming isn't considered analysis is because you typically don't want to overthink or analyze ideas during a brainstorming session. Anyone who's done that knows how quickly it cuts off the flow of creativity. Analysis, while essential at times, has a tendency to interfere with intuition and creativity.

Does "act, then analyze" mean you can't plan ahead? Of course not! Planning and calculating your efforts before investing all of your energy can be critical – especially if you're trying to put a spaceship on the moon and don't want to kill the crew. Realize that even the planning stage requires this type of back and forth energy of action then analysis. It just may be that the "action" could take the form of experimental tests or mental exercises which you then turn around and analyze.

The only real concern of acting without analyzing is doing something dangerous. While this would usually fall under the realm of common sense, I'll go ahead and point out that you'll want to consider these questions:

- Is this dangerous? If so, is the danger realistic or based on irrational fear?
- What's the worst that can *realistically* happen?
- What's the best that can happen?
- Is the benefit worth the risk?

What If I Still Don't Get An Answer?

What do you do if you ask the questions and don't get an answer? Does this mean something is wrong?

Not at all! Not receiving an answer isn't a problem, just like being stuck isn't a problem. It's all a phase in a greater process. We think we ask questions to find answers, but in truth we look for answers so we can find the right questions to ask. Goals (in this case answers) simply act as a catalyst to spur you into action on a journey (asking questions). This is backwards from how we usually think which is that the outcome (goal) is what we're after. As the saying goes, it's about the journey and not the destination. As long as you're alive, the journey (and questions you have) will never end – and it's that fact that actually makes you *feel alive* as opposed to merely existing.

"If the path set before you is clear, you're probably on someone else's." - Joseph Campbell

There were times where I would ask myself "what should I be doing with my life?" I would drive myself crazy because I didn't have a "the" answer. It was only after I realized that this question isn't something you ask once and answer once, that I started to get more clarity. Questions are something to be explored with never-ending curiosity and openness each day. Whatever answers you receive today could change tomorrow when you ask the question again – and this is the way it's meant to be.

What if the point isn't to find the right answers, but to ask the right questions?

Once you can *appreciate* not always having an answer and be OK with it, it's usually at that point that you start to get an answer. It's the resistance to being unclear or confused that keeps you in that state of confusion. The more you welcome the awareness that you won't always get an immediate answer, and appreciate that as an opportunity to explore new possibilities, the more you'll find the answers start to show up.

If you still find yourself in doubt, one thing I've learned from my mentor, Brandon Broadwater, is to shoot for a principle-based solution. What can you do to grow? What can you do to improve your physical or emotional state? What can you do to you serve yourself or another?

You pretty much can't go wrong by developing yourself, serving, or bringing up your state. You'll learn more about how to do these things as the book goes on, but I'm willing to bet you know a number of ways to do these things already. Developing yourself could mean taking on a challenge or practicing a skill. Improving your state could mean listening to uplifting music or saying some positive affirmations. Service can mean giving a friend guidance or telling someone how much you appreciate them. All of these things are go-to targets to look for when you find yourself looking for a step to take.

Chapter 7: How To Break Through Limiting Habits

Once you're aware of what your next step is, or at least have an idea, you now need to consider, "What's holding me back?" You've already identified some limiting vehicles at the end of Chapter 3. Take a moment to consider any other behaviors you believe may be keeping you from your goals. If you're not sure what's holding you back, you'll likely find more insights as you go through this book. You can refer to this chapter at any time as a go-to guide for how to motivate yourself to change your behavior.

The following five-step process is designed to help you "get motivated" enough to adopt a healthier behavior *without* feeling like you're depriving yourself. While it's possible to simply drop an old unhealthy behavior without replacing it with a new behavior, I still recommend having some sort of replacement identity – such as going from "smoker" to "non-smoker."

Let's say someone wants to go to the gym, but find himself too tired after work. He just can't muster up the energy and willpower to get to the gym, so he sits around and watches TV each day telling himself, "Tomorrow I'll start exercising." He'll first find why he's doing what he does now (how it's pleasurable), why he's not doing what he wants to do (why it's painful), and then reframe things so that his current behavior is associated with pain and the new behavior is associated with pleasure.

Step 1: Identify Your Current Behavior's Perceived Benefit
How does my current behavior make me feel?

Whenever I sit at home watching TV, I feel upset with myself for not going to the gym, but I also feel comfortable and relaxed. I feel like watching TV is a good reward for working hard all day. I feel a sense of excitement and fun from watching TV, whereas things would get too boring if I didn't have some evening recreation.

What need(s) is this meeting?

I get certainty/comfort by relaxing. I also feel certainty since watching TV takes no effort and I know I'll enjoy it. I get uncertainty/entertainment because every night it's a different show, and it breaks the mundane aspect of working at my job doing the same thing every day. I get love/connection because I love the TV shows I watch, and becoming engaged with the stories and characters.

Step 2: Identify Your New Desired Behavior's Perceived Detriment
How do I feel when I think about this new behavior?

Going to the gym seems overwhelming. I don't know where to start when I get to the gym and don't know what I'm doing. I also feel intimidated by all the people as if they're watching me and judging me. I hate exercise and it feels like punishment. Part of me wants to do it because I know how much better I'd feel about myself when I get in shape, but another part of me feels it's just not worth the effort.

Note: What you may notice during this step is that when asking yourself how you feel, you may find your reasons for not wanting to do something may not match the story you were originally telling yourself. I often hear people say they don't have the energy to do something, but when digging deeper into how they feel about doing it, they express things like fear and being overwhelmed. In the case of going to the gym, someone may be telling herself she doesn't go because she's tired, but in reality she's actually intimidated by what others may think of her, or confused by all the different exercises and doesn't know where to start. Be sure to really be honest with yourself and notice all the thoughts and feelings inside you when you're imagining doing something.

What need(s) do I feel I'm losing in my life by engaging in this new behavior?

I feel like I'm going to lose my certainty because it's a new environment, it's uncomfortable, and I'm not really sure what I'm doing. I could embarrass myself. I'm going to lose out on entertainment. Watching TV after work is a great way to unwind and enjoy myself, but going to the gym just feels like more work after a long day of work. I also feel like I'm going to lose my significance. I'm usually really good at what I do, but I'm so out of shape that I'm going to feel pathetic trying to do any exercises. I'd rather just not even know how bad it's going to be.

Step 3: Reframe Your Old Behavior
How is this (old) behavior actually causing me to lose things in my life that I really want?

I feel like I'm going to lose my certainty by not having full control over my health. I tend to get sick and my doctor says I need to get in better shape, or I'll be suffering the consequences. I also can't do all the things I wish I could do, and these limitations make me miss out on some of my favorite activities I used to do like play sports (loss of uncertainty/variety). I lose out on love/connection because by sitting around watching TV, because I don't really get to connect with friends, family, and my spouse. I lose out on significance because I'm embarrassed by the shape my body is in, and I know I would feel so much more proud of myself if I got into great shape. I lose out on growth because I'm not developing or maintaining my body's potential, but am actually regressing and backsliding to the point where I may not be able to undo the damage that's done if this goes on much longer.

Step 4: Reframe Your New Behavior
How is this new behavior actually causing me to gain things in my life that I really want?

(Certainty) I feel like I'm going to gain certainty by taking control of my health, and not having to worry so much about disease. I'll feel and look better, and that will give me the extra confidence in other areas of my life. (Excitement) Doing something new like going to the gym and seeing the changes that come from it will be exciting and help break my boring routine. It will be thrilling to see the transformation of my body. (Connection) I will be able to connect and meet new

people at the gym. (Significance) I will gain significance when I see my body change and know that I'm the one responsible. I will feel proud to get myself in better shape than most people are in. (Growth) I will grow by developing my body's potential, and may even find myself enjoying the process of seeing how far I can push my body. Maybe I'll even compete in an athletic competition once I get in better shape just for the fun challenge of it.

Step 5: Make A Choice

Would I rather do this old behavior and get these detrimental results OR would I rather do this new behavior and get these positive results?

Would I rather keep sitting around watching TV, feeling and looking like crap while worried about my health OR would I rather go to the gym, feel great about myself and my body, and experience the excitement of seeing how far I can push myself?

You should create a question that resonates most strongly with both the painful emotions and outcome of the old behavior and the positive emotions and outcome of the new behavior. That means if the thing you fear most is losing your certainty/comfort, you can frame the old behavior in the way that you feel the greatest loss of certainty, and the new behavior in the way the makes you feel the most certainty. If on the other hand, a person's biggest worry was that she's going to lose out on being entertained, then she could focus on how the old behavior causes a loss of entertainment, and/or how the new behavior is also entertaining.

Using Genuine Love, Growth, and Contribution As Motivators

I want to point out that the most potent motivator is that of genuine love. This kind of love is most closely associated with contribution (love for others) and growth (love for yourself) as opposed to the love that's associated with connection – although that's a great motivator too.

I'm talking about a truly selfless love that has another's best interests in mind rather than a more egotistical kind of love. If you can think of a parent that would run into a burning building to save their child, or the challenges you would go through to help a close friend, you understand the power of this kind of selfless love that can inspire action. This kind of motivation will not only help you face inevitable pain, but you may actually *purposely* put yourself through pain for something greater than yourself. Remember that growth and contribution are the two forces you have working in your favor that compel you to accept pain – if for a *greater* purpose.

This means, whenever possible, consider how your actions will reach out to impact others. What if you were doing something for more than just your own sake, but because others were depending on you? What if you could turn your struggles into inspiration for others? What if the love you've been craving from others is really just the love you've been holding back from yourself? What if the work you do to care for and improve yourself is the most loving thing you can do for others?

When it comes to figuring out your big "why" that inspires you, I've found the more you can tie it into how your actions will help and inspire others and yourself, the easier it is to push through the inevitable pain required to go beyond your comfort zone. This also applies to things that are done strictly for personal development and may not seem to really impact others. That's because, whether you like it or not, just your mere presence on this earth *will* impact others. So working on yourself to become your fullest potential is really one of the greatest gifts you can give the world.

Some questions to consider are:

- How could doing this be an act of love for myself?
- How could doing this be an act of love for others?
- How can I turn my experience into inspiration for others?
- Who is depending on me to succeed?
- Why will doing this make the world a better place?

Sustaining Motivation

Once you've made a choice to take on a new behavior, the next challenge you're going to face is maintaining that new behavior against all the obstacles that you're going to face. The key thing to remember is that "success breeds success." If you don't experience an early win and feel the benefits of the new behavior shortly after starting, you may quickly fall back into the old behavior that has served you for so long.

This is known as "creating a positive feedback loop," and it's something Tim Ferriss talks about in his book "The 4-Hour Chef" as being a crucial part of developing any new skill. Imagine a person who tries cooking for the first time and fails miserably. Then after three or four more times, they still haven't experienced success. How motivated do you think they are to stick with it? Compare this to someone who sets the bar fairly low at first to ensure an early victory. They experience the thrilling rush of having a big success right out of the gate. They can then gradually work themselves up to more and more difficult challenges, and still be experiencing success along the way.

There are two ways you can create these early successes to ensure that you stay motivated long enough to stick with a new behavior. The first way is to set challenges for yourself early on that you know you can achieve and then celebrate. This instills a sense of victory, and lets you see the progress you're making. The second way, and this becomes preferable over the long run, is to be consciously aware of the inherent benefits to a behavior so you feel a reward each time you do it.

Sustaining Motivation Method 1: Thirty-Day Challenge And Celebration

Taking our previous example of a person wanting to go to the gym, an outcome-based goal could be something like losing 10 pounds in the first 30 days, or running a 10 minute mile after 30 days. Both of these things give a person something to work towards, and allows them to clearly see the progress being made. It also creates a milestone that a person can celebrate when he reaches it.

By actively celebrating your successes, it reinforces the idea in your head that you're meeting your need of growth. What seems to be a more natural tendency, however, is to downplay our victories and over-emphasize our failures. Whether you succeed or fail, as long as you can tie that into how the experience is helping you grow, you'll still be able to sustain a level of motivation.

When it comes to your first efforts of doing something new, however, you want to make sure you're not setting yourself up to fail *unnecessarily* by taking on too much. My recommended way of doing this is in the form of a 30-day challenge. Thirty days is typically long enough to reinforce a behavior to the point that it becomes habitual. It's also long enough to see tangible results in most things. Naturally, you can adjust this from a 30-day challenge to anything that's appropriate from 3 to 90 days, depending on the activity.

Step 1: Choose The Action You're Looking To Adopt
The first step is to choose a new behavior that is challenging, but easy enough that you know you can do it. Going to the gym seven days a week for an hour a day might be great to work up to, but it's not realistic for a person that hasn't exercised in 20 years. Something like 20 minutes of exercise twice a week might be a better starting point.

Step 2: Choose The Specific Outcome You're Looking To Achieve
The second step is to choose an outcome that is specific and measurable so you know when you've reached it. In the gym example, this could be an exercise goal like lifting a certain amount of weight, or doing a certain number reps, or alternatively, a goal like getting to a particular body weight.

I recommend having an "at least" goal where you can say "I will accomplish at least XYZ or more." For instance, "I will lose at least 10 pounds or more." "I will make at least an extra $200 this month or more." "I will do at least five romantic things or more for my partner.

My favorite types of goals however are based on "just doing it." For instance, just getting to the gym eight times in a month is a victory unto itself – regardless of physical changes. That's fine if you don't want to attach a particular outcome if showing up is big win for you.

Step 3: Get Accountability

Your likelihood of success will be enhanced dramatically if you write this goal down, and share it with someone who will check in with you to see how you're doing. It's very important that this person is supportive and non-judgmental, but will also keep you in check. If you're sufficiently motivated, this isn't always necessary, but if something has been a sticking point for you, then you'll likely find this added accountability is the missing link.

Step 4: Celebrate Your Success

Finally, the fourth step is to celebrate *big time* after the 30 days or when you reach your goal. Pick an activity you can do to treat yourself in order to reinforce your victory. Be willing to work yourself up into a physically excited state during your victory celebration. As down to earth as I am, I have no issues cranking up the music and dancing a victory dance in my room whenever I reach a big goal. Your physiology affects your psychology, and something as simple as dancing, smiling, and jumping up and down (even if you have to force yourself to do it), will help create new neural pathways in your brain to tell it *this* is something important.

This is important because your brain doesn't remember things nearly as well in an emotionally neutral state. If you look back at your past, you probably remember where you were during times of great tragedy or your happiest moments, while you probably don't remember the ordinary mundane situations. We also tend to remember failures more often because pain is a strong emotion. So if you want to connect the feeling of success with the behavior you're adopting, you need to *physically* create a connection with your physiology as best as possible. And if you have physical limitations that prevent moving your body, listening to uplifting music, or closed-eye visualization of yourself in a highly charged state will work.

Finally, remember that you can do a mini-celebration each time you successfully do what you said you were going to do rather than just waiting until after the 30 days. It can be very helpful to reward yourself, even if it's just by giving yourself a smile and telling yourself some words of appreciation, whenever you have *any* success.

Sustaining Motivation Method 2: Enjoying The Experience
While the 30-day challenge is a great tool to create a new habit in your life, focusing on the *inherent* benefits of anything you do (as opposed to just the outcome) is something that I consider to be more foundational and essential to long-term success. This is all about doing something *for its own sake*.

For instance, I rarely eat the right foods, read books, or practice guitar because I'm trying to accomplish any goal; but at one point in time, all those things have felt like work. The reason why these things have taken on an enjoyment all their own has come from creating a strong association with them, and how they meet my needs.

In the earlier exercise, you've already identified how the new behavior you're adopting is meeting your needs. The simple awareness of this alone will help increase your motivation, but the real trick is *staying focused* on those benefits. Anyone who's read a self-help book knows that failures aren't always "bad." The question is, how do you actually remember and appreciate that during the hard times? I've found that it helps to welcome the fact that you're going to make mistakes *before* you make them, and actually develop a healthy sense of looking forward to them as the keys to your further growth and development. That means before setting out on any new endeavor, I expect to make some mistakes and focus more on how I can minimize or overcome them rather than seeing them as a sign that I'm a total screw-up.

The trick of enjoying an experience for its own sake isn't just understanding how something benefits you, it's *remembering* it.

Here are some questions you can be mindful of whenever you're taking on a new behavior:

- If there's something I can love about this, what would it be?
- Why do I appreciate this experience?
- Why do I feel good about doing this?
- How is this helping me grow right now?
- How does doing this align me to my values?
- How does this allow me to better love and serve myself and/or others?
- Why can I welcome and appreciate the mistakes I make?
- How are my setbacks actually moving me forward?

Chapter 8: How To Conquer Self-Sabotage

"He who conquers others is strong; he who conquers himself is mighty." - Lao-Tzu

No matter how motivated and driven you are to do something to better yourself and get unstuck, it's important to understand that you will still feel a force that tries to stop you from doing it. This force that works to keep you stuck, which I and Steven Pressfield in his book "The War Of Art" call "resistance," is not a sign that something is wrong. Experiencing resistance to change or stepping out of your comfort zone is something that you will always experience for the rest of your life. It's the part that wants to avoid any pain and focus only on selfish desires. It's also the force that just wants to maintain the status quo and accept complacency. It's the part of you that says "I just don't feel like it."

For myself, I often feel this resistance when thinking about creating something of value that I can offer to people. This is kind of an inner voice that says things like "Who do you think you are? No one wants what you have to offer. Why bother? You have more important things to do. You're too tired, you deserve a break." Even if what I'm doing is focused on helping others, I still get caught up in my own ego by worrying about letting others down and how *I* would feel about that.

It could be said resistance is the *emotional energy* that is pushing against you whenever you try to get out of a rut. This force wants to keep you in your comfort zone, and prevent you from growing. It especially wants to keep you from doing things that will have a positive impact on the world. Experiencing this resistance is normal, and trying to get rid of it all together isn't likely to work, although there are ways to diminish its impact. What you must learn to do is act in spite of it.

You may be wondering, why would a part of you actually *want* to keep you stuck? Isn't growth a basic need we all have? If you want to do something like improve your relationships, get in better shape, make more money, or do anything else to better your life, why would something inside you (or even other people in the form of *external* resistance) actively work against your own self-development?

Ask yourself, how do muscles grow stronger? Don't they require resistance to work against? How does an athlete improve her performance except by pushing herself beyond what she's comfortable with? Resistance is not something there to keep you stuck. Growth *requires* resistance. Seen in this light, resistance isn't really the enemy. Since everything can enslave or serve you depending on your response to it, resistance can be the very thing you need to develop your inner strength and break through whatever is keeping you stuck.

What if the force trying to stop you from getting what you want is actually the force that's helping you become strong enough to get it?

Identifying Resistance

Resistance will use your emotions against you, and this includes the "positive" emotions. This is why it would be a mistake to simply call resistance "fear," or alternatively call all fear "resistance." While it's true that fear is at the heart of resistance, it may not always show up that way at first. It could just seem like you're "too tired" to do something. Resistance may show up by thinking how much better you'd feel staying up late to watch a movie instead of going to sleep when you need to get up early. We don't necessarily think of these things as fear-based, but it's still a manifestation of resistance when it's keeping you from doing what you need to do.

It's also important to distinguish between genuine fear that serves you well, vs. the type of fear found in resistance. Feeling fear when you come across a dangerous animal, for instance, is helpful to spur you into action. So how do you differentiate between the false fear of resistance vs. a genuine fear that is trying to protect you from real danger? While this takes practicing awareness and learning to be discerning, one simple rule of thumb for myself is to ask whether the "higher," wiser part of me that has my best interest in mind is offering a *counter* resistance/force. In other words, is there a mental/emotional tug-o-war taking place?

In the case of genuine danger, both my emotional and rational mind pretty clearly come together to indicate that getting out of that situation would be wise. However, in the case of feeling resistance to getting work done, there's usually a tug-o-war taking place between a part of me that knows it's in my best interest to do the work, and another part of me that will play any game it can to get me from doing the work.

Once you learn to recognize resistance, it becomes your ally rather than your enemy. When I can identify resistance, it's usually an indicator that whatever I'm feeling resistant to is the *exact* thing I need to do in order to break past my current limitations, assuming there's an intuitive part of me saying "go for it." Seen from this perspective, the stronger the resistance, the more important I know it is to push through that resistance. It acts like a beacon to tell me I'm on the right path.

This happened to me recently I was thinking about offering success coaching. My initial thought was that this would be a great thing to do, and would really help both the students and me improve my coaching skills. Then, right after having that thought, a sinking feeling of anxiety and fear came in telling me not to bother. All kinds of excuses would come up like, "Don't bother. You have plenty of other things to do. What if you screw this up?" What was most startling to me was how these feelings seemed to come out of nowhere and weren't even based on any "real" fear that I had.

In this case, identifying this as resistance just needed a little rational thinking. There was no harm that could come out of coaching someone. If they didn't get what they needed, I could give them their money back. And since there was a strong part of me telling me it was the right thing to do, this tug-o-war was a clear indication that I was dealing with resistance.

I want to point out that there are times where helping someone isn't always the right thing to do if. For instance, if it would enable them to continue down a bad path or sacrifice too much from your own needs. You'll usually find that a wiser part of you knows the right thing to do in these situations or can seek outside assistance. I point this out because resistance can try to keep you from meeting your own needs under the guise of needing to "save the world."

Resistance can take on any number of emotional and rational thought forms. For myself, resistance often takes the form of distraction. It doesn't matter whether it's checking emails, watching YouTube videos, getting on Facebook, or stopping in the middle of writing to go to the kitchen when I'm not even hungry, the underlying method being used is that if resistance can't actually stop me, it's going to slow me down and break my train of thought.

Resistance will almost always use some sort of rationalization to perpetuate itself.

"I need to check my emails instead of getting this work done because maybe there's something important. I need to spend an hour on Facebook because after all, relationships are important. It won't hurt to eat this entire tub of ice cream, for the eleventh night in a row, because I earned it after really breaking a sweat in the gym three weeks ago."

Ask yourself:

- How does resistance show up in my life?
- When does it show up?
- What feelings does it carry with it?
- What methods does it use to take me off track?
- Does it try to get me to do things I know I shouldn't, or does it prefer to simply distract me so that I forget about my priorities?
- Does it try to overwhelm me by slowing but surely getting me to take on too many projects?
- Does it try to get me to procrastinate?
- Does it tell me that I need to get offensive or defensive towards others or myself whenever they push my buttons?

Resistance will use whatever blind spots you have to take you out. If you've ever been able to clearly see the obvious problems with your friends, family, and co-workers that they someone completely miss, realize that you have your own blind spots that the force of resistance will use to take you out. In fact, one of the ways resistance works so well is by hiding itself from you. This is why it's essential to have a coach and supportive people in your life that can offer you feedback on your weak spots. We are *very* good at deceiving ourselves.

If you notice resistance continues in certain areas after you've "caught it," notice what kind of rationalizations it uses to continue its existence. Ask yourself, how am I rationalizing this behavior? Why am I making this OK even when a part of me knows it's not in my best interest?

Overcoming Resistance

The method to overcoming resistance lies in our 3 keys to freedom. Many times, simply shining the light of awareness on the problem helps it going away. By seeing resistance for what it is, it loses much of its power.

The 2nd key is appreciation. We've already discussed why resistance is there to serve you. Rather than fighting it, ask yourself, "why am I grateful for this resistance? How is this helping me become stronger? Why do I need this resistance to reach my fullest potential? How can I turn this resistance into something that will serve me?"

The act of allowing the resistance to be there and *thanking it* takes much of its power away. You'll find that allowance, acceptance, and appreciation dissolves its emotional charge. Taking a note from Emotional Freedom Technique, you can say a mantra like "even though I feel this resistance, I still deeply and completely love and accept myself." If you can appreciate that resistance is helping you meet your need of growth, it no longer becomes your enemy, but more like a weight in the gym you *purposely* use to strengthen your emotional and mental muscles.

Finally, you'll need the 3rd key to overcome resistance, which is to take action in spite of it. What you'll find is that whenever you act in spite of your resistance, gradually the resistance diminishes in that area. For instance, when I first started coaching people, it was a scary experience that I felt some resistance to. Then over time, by acting in spite of my fear, I found it gradually subsided.

This doesn't mean you won't continue to experience some resistance in various areas of your life no matter how much you act in spite of it. You may overcome resistance in one area, but it will likely show up in another area. The good news is that the more you learn to act in spite of resistance, the easier *everything* becomes. This is because you gain an awareness and appreciation for how to use the force of resistance to actually propel you through your sticking points. The very thing that was holding you back becomes a force that pushes you forward.

The best way I know of to act in spite of resistance is to step outside of your own ego and focus on genuine love for another. How many fears would you be able to overcome if the life of someone you loved depended on it? The thing is, many people are depending on you, whether you realize it or not, to step into your fullest potential. If you can mentally connect how acting in spite of your resistance or fear is in the best interest of both yourself and others, then you'll find your ability to move forward becomes significantly easier.

For myself, whenever I'm feeling resistant to something, it's almost always because I'm worried about how it's going to impact me. As soon as I put myself in some else's shoes and think about how my actions can positively impact them, the resistance is greatly diminished. At the very least, I'm able to act in spite of it. If fear is stopping you, it's not because of too much fear – it's because of failing to focus enough on whom and what you love.

The easiest way to overcome fear is to get off your own agenda and focus on another's.

Some questions you can ask to overcome resistance are:

- Do I want to let this have power over me, or would I rather make a choice in my best interest?

- Why will I feel more fulfilled taking this action?
- Would I rather succumb to my fear or act from love?
- Why does loving myself require I take this action?
- Why does loving others require I take this action?
- If people are depending on me, even if I don't realize it, how does taking this action help them?
- How does doing this for myself serve others in the long run?
- What if people are waiting for my example? Do I want to let them down, or prove to them how much I love them?

Willpower Strengthening

No matter how inspired and motivated you are, there's no getting around the fact that sometimes you just won't feel like doing something. This is especially true when you first start to work on changing a long-standing habit. Even with the various exercises and techniques laid out in this book to help "get you motivated," it still takes your willpower to read the book and go through the exercises.

While relying on willpower to get yourself to do everything would quickly drain you, there's a good chance you're going to need willpower to get the ball rolling initially. The way I look at it, changing your mindset is like greasing a path that you're going to have to roll the ball down. To get that ball moving, you still have to make that initial push.

The good news is you can train yourself to act in spite of resistance and develop greater willpower. A simple technique for this is, whenever you feel inspired to do something, take some sort of action within five seconds of getting the impulse. If you don't overcome that initial resistance within the first few seconds, there's a very good chance you'll talk yourself out of it.

While the 30-day challenge is designed to help you develop the willpower to take on a new habit without overwhelming yourself, there's another practice that I believe to be highly beneficial for anyone looking to not only develop their willpower, but get a few other health benefits too. That is taking ice cold showers.

If you're cringing at the idea, then great! That is exactly what you want. I started taking cold showers exclusively and find them to be a great way to train myself to overcome resistance. As a side note, cold showers boost the immune system and may even be somewhat beneficial for fat loss.

Whenever I'm about to turn on the water, I can feel in my gut the part of me that screams not to do it. I can hear the voices in my head making excuses. I see, feel, and hear exactly what kind of form my resistance takes inside of me. Since logically I know there's no harm that will come to me, it's a useful practice to help me distinguish between resistance and genuine fear.

Nevertheless, you may find yourself trying to think of reasons why this is stupid. "Some guy in a book says to take cold showers... what an idiot! Why should I do that? I don't need to take cold showers to prove anything to myself. I have plenty of willpower already. Even if I don't, this isn't the way to get it." And so on....

This is exactly what resistance does. It makes you feel like not doing something, and then use rationalizations and excuses to justify that feeling. The reason why taking cold showers is important is not because you literally *need* to take cold showers, but because it's a safe and effective way to both identify what resistance feels like and train yourself to act in spite of it. The other reason why it's great is because you'll find after a few moments, the initial pain and resistance wears off. In fact, most of the pain is just in agonizing over the experience before-hand. The less time you take to just jump right in, the easier it is. Overtime your body will adapt to the cold, and it won't feel so bad.

I've made it my goal to take ice cold showers each day with as little hesitation as possible. The idea is to just jump right in the shower and do it, so I give myself no more than five seconds to take action. The other great thing about cold showers is that, despite them becoming more enjoyable over time, they always kind of suck – for me at least. This means every day you can do something that will break you out of your comfort zone. Every day, you'll take one action in spite of resistance, and this will train that part of your brain that forces you to act when you don't feel like it.

Naturally, the idea is to then transfer this experience to every area of your life. Whenever you feel resistance, remember that it's just like jumping into a cold shower. It will feel bad at first, but then you get used to it. The worst part is agonizing over it. If you don't give yourself time to think about it, and just do it without hesitation, you'll find it's almost never as bad as you think it is.

Chapter 9: How To Change Limiting Perceptions

It's easy to understand that your perception of things creates your experience. If you change your perception, you change your experience of the world. If you don't get this, then ask yourself, "Would I have any problems if I only thought happy thoughts?" Granted, the point isn't to only think happy thoughts. However, by changing your perception, you can make better choices to make real, tangible changes in your life. For the things you can't change in the world, changing your perception gives you the ability to be at peace with what is.

In order to change your perception to something more empowering, you must first understand what's holding your perception in place. What's keeping your perception fixed are your beliefs, many of which aren't really right or wrong, but are viewpoints you've adopted and continue to hold onto.

Let's look at an example at how beliefs and thoughts work together to create perception. I worked for a number of years in customer service jobs where I interacted with customers who could be incredibly rude and disrespectful at times. This made it very easy to adopt the belief that "people are rude" or even just "many people are rude."

Once a person adopts a belief, their brain is designed to confirm this belief by filtering out anything contrary to that belief, and highlighting all the instances where it's true (or seems true). What this means is that even though a person with the belief that "people are rude" may deal with 20 people in a day of which 19 are all perfectly normal and respectful, they'll tend to not think about them if they've had one really rude customer. They won't say, "Today was great because I dealt with 19 really nice people." Instead, all they'll be able to think about was the *one* rude person. They'll sit back and go, "See, people are so rude! I know I'm right because look at how rude that person was to me!" The person is overlooking all the experiences to the contrary because their brain filters out that which doesn't match their beliefs.

The way a belief is reinforced and lives on is that the brain is constantly running phrases and questions like "Why is everyone so rude? When am I going to have to deal with the next jerk? I can't believe how disrespectful some people are." These phrases and questions play like a soundtrack on repeat in the background of a person's mind, directing their focus to find every single instance of rudeness, which it then highlights and emphasizes in the person's awareness.

Even if you don't hold the belief that people are rude, can you think of a belief you do have that's really a subjective opinion? How readily can you think of things that confirm that belief for you? Now, how readily can you think of things that directly contradict that belief? Chances are, your mind is filled with examples you can draw upon to confirm a belief, but has a much harder time finding contradictory information. That's not because it doesn't exist, it's because your brain has filtered it out of your awareness so it doesn't have to deal with contradictions.

The other important thing to understand about beliefs is that any belief you've adopted is something that has benefited you in some way. That means it meets one or more of your six human needs. This may sound strange at first because people can have all sorts of screwed up beliefs that seem to be purely destructive. For instance, a person may believe "no one loves me." By looking more closely however, you can see that a person may hold onto this belief because it gives them certainty. Phrasing it as "everyone hates me" would clearly show how this belief gives that person significance.

Of course, we're not usually conscious of when we've adopted beliefs, why we've adopted them, and to an even lesser degree, how to let them go. The short answer is that many beliefs get programmed into us when we were children and didn't have the conscious discernment to choose whether or not to accept or reject what we experienced. We then grew up holding onto all sorts of beliefs that may have even benefitted us at one time, like never talk to strangers, but no longer make any sense later in life.

If your beliefs are keeping you stuck (and it's almost a guarantee that at some point, some of your beliefs will), then it's going to be necessary to identify those beliefs and replace them with more empowering beliefs that will serve you better than the old beliefs.

Changing Your Beliefs

There are any number of psychological methods to identify and change your beliefs such as hypnosis, NLP, EFT, emotional releasing, and more. For very deep-seated beliefs and addictions, I always recommend seeing a qualified professional. It can be nearly impossible to work through some things by oneself. Either way, realize that releasing old beliefs can be considered an ongoing process. Sometimes sudden changes in beliefs can be very hard to deal with and integrate into your life, so this long-term approach isn't necessarily a bad thing as it helps you make adjustments gradually.

Here is a simple, five-step formula that you can use to start working on overcoming limiting beliefs:

1. Identify a current belief and accept it;
2. Be willing to let it go;
3. Choose a new perspective;
4. Adopt a new perspective;
5. Reinforce the new perspective;

Step 1: Identify Current Beliefs

The reason this book starts out with mindfulness is because it is such a great practice to uncover many of the beliefs that are holding you back. These could be things like "I don't know what to do," "I'll never be happy," or "I'm not good enough." They could also be related to specific issues you're facing. If a person has challenges with finances, they may believe: "There's never enough money." "I'm not smart enough to start my own business." "Rich people are evil, and I don't want to be evil."

Remember that a particular belief might have been very beneficial at one point in time, but now it could be holding you back. Some examples from my own life include "I have to exercise at least 3 hours a week to get in shape," "If I don't help everyone I can, people won't like me," "Working harder is the only way to succeed." This means letting go of thinking of beliefs as good or bad, but rather whether or not they're currently empowering you or disempowering you to do what's best.

Ask: What beliefs are holding me back?

You may find you already know the answer to this question. If so, great! But if not, here are some suggestions to help you dig deeper to uncover limiting beliefs.

- Try using the phrase: "XYZ is keeping me stuck," and see what your first instinct is to put in there. Write down as many ideas as you come up with, and pick whatever belief or beliefs resonate with you the most. *Examples: "I'm not motivated, and it's keeping me stuck." "I don't know what to do, and it's keeping me stuck." "Other people criticize me, and it's keeping me stuck."*
- Look for statements that use the extremes like all/none, must/can't, never/always, no one/everyone. *Examples: "Everyone thinks I'm stupid." "All men are selfish." "There's never enough money." "There are no good jobs."*
- When thinking about something you like to do, ask why you can't do it. The excuse that follows the "because" is your limiting belief. *Examples: "I can't fix my marriage, because my husband is crazy." "I'll never be successful, because I didn't get a good education."*
- Ask yourself; if your excuse was no longer relevant, would you definitely take the desired action? *Examples: "I can't exercise, because I don't have the time." "If I did have the time, say an extra 30 minutes a day, would I start to exercise? Actually, no. I'd probably keep watching re-runs of Jersey Shore. So what really is the problem? I believe if I get in shape my friends will be jealous of me, and it would make them feel bad about their own poor health."*

Even if you don't have any particular limiting beliefs at the moment, then you can work on the following.

Old disempowering belief: **"My challenges are a problem, and keep me stuck."**

New empowering: **"My challenges can either serve or enslave me, and I have the free will to choose which."**

Step 2: Be Willing To Let It Go

Even in the cases of the most destructive and disempowering beliefs, it can be difficult to want to let go of long-standing beliefs. While on a conscious level you may love to get rid of disempowering thoughts and beliefs, remember that on an subconscious level, each one of your beliefs has been adopted because it seemed to benefit you in some way. Whether or not it *actually* benefited you is irrelevant. The point is that on an emotional level you usually feel it's more comfortable to have that belief than not have it – unless you've experienced the alternative.

The one benefit that all beliefs have in common, no matter how crazy they are, is they give you certainty. This explains why people can become extremely upset, defensive, and fanatical when their beliefs are questioned. To challenge a person's beliefs, particularly their core beliefs, may be tearing away at the only things they have giving them certainty in life.

It's also important to understand this because as you let go of long-standing beliefs, you'll find two things start to happen due to losing certainty. The first thing is life takes on a more dreamlike quality. This may sound strange at first, but it makes sense when you consider that most of what makes reality seem objective is your beliefs telling you how things are or aren't. This is, for most people, both exciting and scary. The other thing that happens is that you find yourself feel more united and harmonized with others. The walls of differing beliefs are torn down and you'll find yourself better able to see multiple points of view without attaching to any of them.

Because this can be a new and uncomfortable experience, we often don't want to face our beliefs and release them no matter how limiting they are. As stated earlier, "better the devil you know than the devil you don't" is the mantra of those who crave certainty. Remember, we *all* crave certainty to some degree or another. To let go of old beliefs and perspectives requires taking a plunge into uncertainty.

So how do you work up the courage to face the uncertainty? As Tony Robbins says, most people change when the pain of staying the same outweighs the pain of change. If this is the point you're at in a belief, then you'll probably already be willing to make the change no matter what kind of uncertainty you're going to face. However, if you're not at the point of being in so much pain that you *have to* change, then you need the ability to envision something greater than you have now to such a degree that it will push you through any uncertainty. This can be as simple as recognizing how your old belief isn't helping you, and then seeing a better belief that can take its place. In the vast majority of cases, this comes from seeing and being inspired by *others* who've adopted a more empowering perspective, which in turns shows you a new possibility for your own life. I would go so far as to say if you did nothing else except hang out with people who are living a life like you'd like to live, that alone will have the effect of absorbing and adopting their beliefs and attitude by exposure.

Each of these things, pain and hope (pleasure), are powerful motivators. The third and most powerful motivator of all is love. When your love for yourself and others *demands* that you become someone greater by shedding old beliefs and taking on a more empowered perspective, then you will become unstoppable.

Questions To Help Let Go:
- What will happen in a year if this doesn't change?
- What will happen in five years if this doesn't change?
- Can I absolutely know this belief is true?
- Is there anyone for whom this belief isn't true?
- Why will I be OK without this belief?
- Why do I deeply and completely love and accept myself with or without this belief?

- What would a more empowering belief look like? Would I rather have my old belief or this new empowering belief?
- Can I let it go?
- If I could let it go, would I?
- Why does loving myself mean letting go of this?
- Why does loving others mean letting go of this?
- Why will my life be much better letting go of this?

Step 3: Choose A New Empowering Perspective

While you're more than welcome to adopt any particular belief you believe will empower you, I do have some suggestions based on my experience. My experience is that going to either extreme, be it positive or negative, can have unintended consequences. Instead, I believe the wisest path is that of the middle road.

To see what this looks like on a practical level, let's say someone has the belief "everyone hates me." Obviously, this is a pretty disempowering belief that's going to lead to things like depression. The natural tendency is to want to replace that with a belief like "everyone loves me." This would be the typical approach for positive thinking-fluffy-feel good type of self-help stuff. While this belief is more empowering and likely to lead to a better quality of life, it's still not the *most* empowering. Remember, empowering isn't the same as "positive." The reasons why it's not the most empowering belief are because 1) it's probably not true and eventually there's going to be evidence to the contrary and 2) it's putting a person's happiness into other people's hands. In other words, the belief is centered around something a person has no control over - other people's opinion and feelings. Also consider that a person who believes "everyone loves me" could turn into an arrogant jerk who may do whatever they please because they believe they can do no wrong.

So what is an empowering belief that could be used here? One suggestion would be something like *"No matter* whether people love me or hate me, *I'm still ok and I deeply love and accept myself and love and accept them."* Another option could be *"Some people will love me, some people will hate me, but no matter what I love myself."* These beliefs are both more empowering as well as more *realistic*.

The first thing this type of belief does is it recognizes the truth of the matter. Some people are going to hate you and that's fine. It's only a problem if you choose to make it your problem. The empowered person isn't the person whom everyone loves, it's the person who can be OK with themselves no matter what others think. They control their own reality.

Another example of a "false" empowering belief is "if someone dislikes me, there's something wrong with them." While this may once again appear to be better than getting down on yourself if someone's opinion of you isn't favorable, it still locks you into a game of "I'm right, they're wrong." This is a game that will always rob you of your power, because it will set you against the outside world. Remember, the truly empowered person remains unaffected by others' opinions.

In this case, where the negative bias is projected onto others rather than yourself, I would adopt a belief like "Whether they love or hate me, *they're* still ok." With this belief, you release any judgment towards others because of a bias they may have. You'll never have others embrace you without judgment until you first release your judgment towards them. In essence, this is an act of forgiveness and compassion.

While I'm using the example of beliefs centered around being loved, the idea here is to adopt realistic and truly empowering beliefs. True empowerment could be summed up as the ability to choose to be OK with whatever is here right now without having to force things to be different. It's a state of non-attachment and non-resistance to anything other than what is in the present moment. To reach that point, it begins with an appreciation and acceptance of how all things can be serving you for your highest good.

Recommended Empowering Perspectives

Here are some empowering perspectives that are foundational to helping you move forward and get out of any rut.

- I am 100% responsible for my life and my experience.
- I am grateful for every challenge I face as it helps me grow.
- No matter what, I am OK and I completely love and accept myself.
- I welcome all my emotions as helpful guides, and all my feelings have a right to live.
- I have all the resources I need within me now.

Finding A New Empowering Perspective

1. What is my old disempowering belief?
2. How did that belief benefit me? Which of the six human needs did it meet?
3. Is there a more empowering belief that will meet those same needs?

Let's take a look at one of the most disempowering beliefs a person can have – "I'm a victim." Right now I'm being purposely vague because we all probably have some area of our life where we feel like a victim. If you want to know what this looks like, just ask yourself if you've ever felt sorry for yourself, complained, or blamed anyone or anything. If so, this is playing the role of a victim.

You may believe that you're a victim in a more general sense in that life seems to really enjoy screwing you over time and time again. Perhaps you just can't wrap your mind around being OK with the tragic circumstances you find yourself in, and even find the idea offensive. You might not understand how you can keep your cool if someone blatantly disrespects you. Maybe you're someone who has prided themselves on always recognizing the power of your thoughts to influence your perception, but just can't seem to shake the negative thoughts surrounding a recent experience.

Whether or not any of those things apply to you, there will always be times when we want to be the "victim," even if this is a belief that takes power away from ourselves and gives it to others (disempowering). Sometimes there's no arguing that bad stuff happens, and you'd rather just take a bit of time to feel sorry for yourself and have others feel sorry for you too. After all, being a victim is a great way to meet your needs of certainty (I'm right, they're wrong), uncertainty (I have no control over my life and anything could happen), love (I get sympathy from others), and significance (this happened to ME).

Being a victim does make us feel better in some way. If we didn't get benefits out of being a victim, we wouldn't tell ourselves that story – and if you haven't noticed, it's a very popular story.

In a short-term sense, playing the role of a victim can be OK. The question is, does adopting a victim perspective serve you more than an alternative perspective over the long haul? Let's compare the difference between an individual who lives with a victim perspective vs. someone who believes they are responsible for their experience.

Victim Pros:

- Gain certainty: Gets to be right, and either the world or others are wrong.
- Gain uncertainty: Gets to let go of responsibility allowing for greater freedom – no need to try to control or change anything.
- Gain love: Gets to connect with others through complaining. Gets sympathy and affection from people.
- Gain significance: Gets attention – particularly when acting overly dramatic about the situation. Gets to feel important.

Victim Cons:

- Lose certainty: No control over one's experience. Lacks inner confidence and hope.
- Lose uncertainty: Loses the freedom to live a life of choice.
- Lose love: Can't form deeper connections through compassion and selfless love.

- Lose significance: Not likely to be successful. People won't admire or respect victims as much.
- Lose growth: Can't overcome resistance but is crushed by it. Stays stuck or regresses at a current level of psychological, spiritual, and/or physical development.
- Lose contribution: Too worried about own problems to help others.

Responsible Pros:

- Gain certainty: Has the ability to dictate one's own perception. Has an "I can handle anything" confident perspective.
- Gain uncertainty: Gains freedom through discipline. Can do more exciting things without risking as much certainty.
- Gain love: Gets to feel love by drawing it from within rather than taking it from others. Gives love to self and others and therefore receives it in return.
- Gain significance: More responsibility equals more success. The most successful, respected, and admired people are those who've taken responsibility.
- Gain growth: Accepts challenges as opportunities to learn and grow. Sees the lessons in everything and learns from mistakes.
- Gain contribution: Uses experiences as motivation to create positive change. Has the ability to actually make a difference.

Responsible Cons:

- Lose certainty: Doesn't get to be "right" by making others wrong.
- Lose uncertainty: Doesn't experience the excitement of manufactured "drama."
- Lose love: Doesn't get pity from others.
- Lose significance: Doesn't get attention without having to command it.

At first it may seem paradoxical that these things can cause both an increase and a decrease in the same needs like certainty. Most beliefs act like a double-edged sword, where things are constantly in a state of compromise. Even if one perspective, like taking responsibility, meets more of your needs than being a victim, it does so at the expense of being more difficult or more delayed in the positive outcome. Just like some people prefer the finer things in life and are willing to pay a higher price for them while others prefer what's cheaper and easier to acquire, it's the same with the attitudes we adopt in terms of the compromises we make.

You'll also find paradoxes within a single point. For instance, "gaining freedom through discipline" may seem like a contradictory statement. How does being more disciplined and responsible increase your freedom when discipline and responsibility seem to be all about restriction and limitation?

Freedom can be looked at a number of ways. In the instant gratification mindset, it's seen as the ability to do whatever you want. However, since the world we live in doesn't let you do whatever you want without consequence, is this really freedom? An example I like to give of how this works is a person's diet and how that affects their freedom. A person may have the freedom as an adult to choose to eat only doughnuts for every meal of every day. Eventually, however, that freedom will lead to them losing the freedom that comes with having a healthy body. They'll end up with sickness and physical problems that may interfere with their work or passions. They'll end up lacking energy and feeling like crap all the time. If their diet isn't fixed, they may even face the ultimate loss of freedom – death.

You may have freedom of choice, but not freedom to choose a different consequence for a choice.

On the contrary, someone who practices discipline with their diet may lose out on a short term freedom like getting to eat whatever they feel like. What they will gain is the freedom that comes with having a healthier body; a body that has the energy to do more fun activities and doesn't have to worry about sickness stopping someone as often from doing whatever she wants to do.

So it is with all of our perspectives and beliefs. We're constantly trading one thing for another. This means the only really "true" freedom comes when you can let go of needing all the external stuff to satisfy all the internal stuff.

Finding A New Empowering Perspective Technique: Hero's Journey Story

While there are very few beliefs or viewpoints I would ever want to force on someone, there is a universal belief and understanding that seems to be hardwired into every single human being. This is something that we intuitively understand and appreciate so much, that it is the basis of almost every single story, from ancient myths to modern movies, books, and television stories. All these stories that resonate with us follow a similar pattern which teach a similar lesson – we must overcome challenges to reach our fullest potential. You must face opposition to be a hero, and we're all called to rise up and be heroes in our own way, or else be crushed by the inevitable opposition in your life.

The pattern in all these stories is the Hero's Journey – also called the monomyth. While there are various outlines created for the Hero's Journey, I'll simply describe the overall process. The protagonist in a story in which the protagonist has an ordinary life, then some dramatic event calls them to adventure, they undergo trials and tribulations, then when all seems lost, they overcome their challenges and are transformed in the process. When they return "home" or the adventure ends, the hero and/or the rest of the world is better for it.

Whether it's Luke Skywalker in Star Wars, Dorothy in the Wizard of Oz, James Bond, or any other character you can think of in stories that resonate with a mass of people, the formula is more or less the same. The take-home points are that it's through his challenges that he is transformed, and at the end, he has a prize that he didn't have before.

If you try to think of any stories that are extremely compelling that don't have any challenge, struggle, or problems that must overcome, you'll find there aren't too many. Most people see stories without conflict as somewhat boring due to the lack of "movement." In other words, in order for the protagonist to end up in a better spot than where they started, they *need* some sort of challenge (antagonist), be it an external adversary or an internal one, to overcome.

The reason the Hero's Journey speaks to us is because we're all on our own Hero's Journey. No matter what form the hero takes in a story, we can always relate to her on some level. We can imagine the difficulty of her trials, and we want to root her on to victory and see her overcome her obstacles. This isn't something that's taught to us or instilled in us like other belief systems. It's something that speaks to the core of who we are as human beings.

There's always an important point in the Hero's Journey, and that is when the Hero first refuses the call to action. She doesn't want to face the struggles, and naturally she'll turn away. In the stories, something or someone compels her to act in spite of her resistance. In real life, the trials and challenges come whether you like it or not, but whether they transform you into a Hero or beat you down into submission is based on your free will. You can always choose to reject that call because your story is your creation.

What you're going to do with this technique is use your "what if" imagination so you can craft your own Hero's Journey story based on the challenges you're facing. Imagine you're writing a story where the hero is going through whatever challenge you're facing, or whatever challenge you've gone through in the past and can't see the benefits of. You're going to ask yourself, "Why did the hero *have to* go through this?" and "What happens later in the hero's life that made this challenge absolutely *necessary* so they were prepared for what was to come?" You'll then make up a future situation in which the hero's previous struggles were the *key* to their ultimate success and triumph.

Let's make up a story to see how this would play out. Let's say you had just started a business with a partner, and the partner lied to you, cheated you out of your money, and left you broke. Under the current circumstances, looking at the bright side of things might not immediately bring much relief to the money situation, but after the initial anger and depression wears off, you're going to need to pick yourself up.

If this happened, we could start the story with "Jane," who had this happen to her. So using the power of imagination, you'd come up with a situation down the road where Jane uses this experience to her advantage.

Thinking of just a few examples, Jane may end up:

- Writing a book and become a speaker on how to pick the right business partners.
- Learning the signs of deception, and uses that to help a member of her family avoid a similar fate in a relationship of theirs.
- Working her way out of debt, and then start a new business that helps other people get out of debt that ends up being far more successful than her original business may have ever been.

Whatever situation you come up with, it should compensate for the initial challenge of the hero. Even if nothing makes it up to the hero, then at least *the rest of the world* gets the benefit. Nearly everything that inspires us follows this pattern. Parents lose a child to a disease, and they start a charity that helps save thousands of other kids from the same fate. A person loses a limb in an accident, but still lives his dreams and inspires others to do the same. A person loses all their possessions only to find true happiness without needing material things – and then perhaps striking it rich later on as a bonus too.

Now from a practical standpoint, the actual likelihood of things playing out in your real life like they do in your made-up story are slim. That's not the purpose of the exercise. Rather, it's to direct your mind to find the lessons the hero needed to learn from the challenge. The point of the hero's journey is not the ending. It's the *transformation* that takes place within the hero. It's seeing the lessons she learned and the way she grew through the challenges that resonates with us when hearing these stories.

So now you ask questions like:

- How did this experience transform the hero for the better?
- How did this experience transform others for the better?
- What was the most important lesson for the hero?
- How did the situation end up empowering and freeing the hero, rather than enslaving him?
- Why would the hero look back and be grateful for the challenge?
- What solution was waiting to be manifested within the problem?
- How did the dark experience they went through create a brighter future?
- If this challenge *had to* happen for a greater good, what would that greater good be?

And as your mind looks for the benefits in your made-up story, so will you find the benefits in your own situation. Remember that all the various stories we love have many different characters, situations, and endings. The actual details don't matter, it's the *internal* transformation and lessons learned that we all relate to.

The temptation might be to say, "Well, I'm just making this story up, it doesn't necessarily mean that's *my* story." The thing is, no matter what your current story you're telling yourself about your life and situation is, you made that up too. So if you're going to be making up stories for yourself anyways, why not make it a good one?

Whatever story you tell yourself about your life is completely made up by your imagination, so why not imagine a better story?

Step 4: Adopt A New Perspective
The problem with a lot of self-help advice is that, although it's well-meaning, it often tries to force change by telling people how they "should" think or feel. If you've ever been feeling down and had someone tell you "don't worry" or "look on the bright side," then you know how frustrating this can be. Their easy comeback fails to honor the legitimacy of your current feelings. In a sense, it's like saying "you're wrong" for feeling

the way you feel. And even if others don't say it, there's a good chance you're saying things to yourself about how you need to think and feel differently than you do.

Forcing a perspective, be it to feel a certain way or not feel something doesn't work – at least not in the long run. What you resist, persists. Burying your negative emotions, and then trying to force positive feelings on top, can actually lead to more damage down the road. Instead, we need to welcome and allow both your current thoughts and perspective as well as any more empowering alternatives. Releasing anything, such as sadness, anger, anxiety, depression, or feeling stuck and confused, begins with welcoming and honoring the feelings.

You can't let go of what's no longer serving you until you've welcomed it in and allowed it to have its say.

There are a couple techniques that I've found to be helpful in allowing yourself to welcome a new perspective with ease rather than force. They are what I call "what if?" and "try it out."

Step 4: Adopt A New Perspective, Method 1: What If?
In times where my faith was shaken or non-existent, I found another lifeline to pull me out – curious imagination. This means adopting a "what if" type of attitude towards whatever you're resisting. For instance, if a person couldn't possibly believe losing his job could serve him in some way, he doesn't necessarily have to believe it. He just needs to imagine the idea that it *could* be true and see how that feels.

You could ask:

- If there was a good reason for this, what *might* it be?
- If this could serve me in some way, how *might* that be?"
- If there was something to be grateful for in this situation, what would it be?
- If I could let these feelings go, *just for now*, would I?
- If I wasn't a victim, what would I be thinking and feeling right now?

- If I was completely empowered right now, what would that look like?
- If there was a different "truth" that was better than what I believe now, what might it be?
- If I knew this situation was actually serving me, how would I feel and respond?
- If I'm responsible for my experience, what experience would I choose right now?
- What if something amazing is going to come from this?
- What if this experience is exactly what I need to make a big breakthrough?

The beauty of these questions is that they don't necessarily require you to have faith that there is any sort of "higher purpose" behind it all, if that's all a little too airy-fairy for your tastes. Instead, they only require you to use your imagination and simply *make up* a benefit. And when you direct your mind to start looking for lessons, it will find them. Maybe not at first, but if you keep asking the question with a genuine curiosity, and simply allow yourself to create a story about how it's benefiting you, then you'll get the lesson.

If you don't yet have faith, have curiosity.

One of the best examples from my life of turning a bad situation into something good was when I applied for college. I was too late in getting in a submission, and I was told that I would have to wait until next semester. This devastated me, and I was in a rage. I had worked so hard to get everything together, but was now being told I would have to wait.

While a part of me knew it could be happening for a good reason, I just couldn't understand what it would be. So instead of waiting for some sort of divine heavenly light to shine down and show me the good that was to come of this, I made up my own lesson. While I'm not sure exactly what I asked myself at the time, I'm sure it was something along the lines of "What could I do to turn this into something good? If there was something good to come of this, what might it be?"

By simply activating my imagination and looking for a way to turn it into something good, I realized I could go to a college in my home town to take all of my core classes, then attend my desired college starting my sophomore where I was going to get my music degree. The more I thought about it, the more I realized this was actually a much smarter decision. I would save a significant amount of money by attending a cheaper college for a year and living with my parents. A few days later, I got an email from the college I originally wanted to attend telling me the "good news" that some student had dropped out, and they could accept me into the program that Fall. I happily declined and said I would be attending the following year.

"Every challenge we face in life exists so we can manifest its *solution.*" Dr. Vernon Woolf

Step 4: Adopt A New Perspective, Method 2: Try It Out
The technique that I call "try it out" is a form of welcoming and non-resistance. It's set up in such a way that you don't feel like you really have to let go of your old perspective if you don't want to. This approach of trying out a different perspective is especially significant when you're really attached to whatever story you're telling yourself and find it next to impossible to adopt a different perspective.

Let's say someone was cheated on by a spouse, and now can't possibly imagine feeling anything other than anger, resentment, and ultimately, like a victim of mistreatment. The first step to trying it out a new perspective is to first welcome and accept the current state. This could mean acknowledging thoughts and feelings like "I feel hurt. I feel like there's no possible way I can get through this. I feel like I've been victimized."

Then, ask yourself "Just for now, could I welcome another perspective?" The idea here is that you can, if only for the next minute or two, "try out" a perspective that is more empowering. This is a technique I learned from the Sedona Method, something I highly encourage you to check out. You can always go back to feeling like how you felt before, but you're going to take just a moment to experience something else. In other words, it's sort of like saying "I am a victim, but just for the next few minutes, I'm going to experience things like I'm not, and see how that would feel. Then afterwards I'll go back to being a victim if I want to."

To do this, use an "if" questions and/or the phrase "just for now" and allow yourself to imagine a different reality for yourself only for the current moment. Remember, you don't have to keep this perspective, but just "try it out." You can always go back to your old perspective.

- Could I, just for now, let go of whatever I'm resisting?
- Could I, just for now, let go of whatever I'm attached to?
- Could I, just for now, adopt a different perspective?
- If I could let these disempowering feelings go, just for now, would I?
- If right now I wasn't a victim, what would I be thinking and feeling?
- If I was completely empowered just for now, what would that look like?
- Could I, just for now, experience what it's like to feel free?

If a certain part of you wants to fight this and say, "This isn't really true, I'm just making stuff up!" Then simply welcome and honor that. Remember, if that's the perspective you want to live by, you're free to continue to hold onto that after the exercise is done. For now, we're just "trying out" a new perspective. You're adopting the role of a child who's imagining that things are different, and then experiencing life from that perspective, if for only a moment.

If you find yourself ready to move on to a more empowering perspective, all you need to do is let go of the old, and welcome the new. Some questions that can help are:

- **Can I welcome my current thoughts and feelings?**
- **Can I thank them for serving me?**

- **Can I let go of this?** *Examples: Can I let go of this anger? Can I let go of feeling like a victim? Can I let go of wanting to control others? Can I let go needing approval?*
- **Would I rather have this or something better?** *Examples: Would I rather feel like a victim, or feel empowered? Would I rather feel angry, or feel at peace? Would I rather hold onto this resentment, or forgive myself/them?*
- **Can I welcome this new perspective?** *Examples: Can I welcome this responsibility? Can I welcome this peace? Can I welcome how my challenges serve me?*

I should note, this isn't necessarily an instant process, although it can be. You may want to repeat these steps each day to gradually let go, and introduce new perspectives. Then reinforce the new perspective with the following techniques.

Step 5: Reinforce A New Perspective, Method 1: Behavior

Even if you've mentally accepted a new mindset and outlook on life, the next challenge is to actually overcome your tendency to fall back into old patterns. Your thoughts and feelings can become habitual just like any external behavior. In other words, sometimes the biggest difficulty in letting go of an old way of seeing things is that you're just too used to it.

While it's true that your inner thoughts will affect your actions, the reverse is also true. That is, changing your actions will influence your thinking. It works both ways. Research has shown that a person's posture affects their hormone levels which then in turn affect how a person feels. Even forcing a smile has the effect of actually making you feel better. This means just moving your body differently will literally affect the hormones, endorphins, and thought processes taking place inside of you.

The first way of adopting and reinforcing a new perspective is to "act as if" you already have the desired mindset and outcome. If you want to be more financially successful, for instance, you act as if you already are financially successful. This doesn't necessarily mean buying stuff you can't afford, but it may mean getting rid of old junk, donating money to charity (because you believe you'll make more), dressing in nicer clothes, and carrying yourself with a posture of a person sure of themselves.

At first, this may seem to contradict the notion that you shouldn't "force" things – which by the way is somewhat of a half-truth. Some people shy away from the "fake it til you make it" approach because it seems disingenuous. There's an element of truth that faking things is really just addressing a symptom and not the root problem – a disempowering mindset. However, assuming you've done the inner work which includes releasing old beliefs and welcoming new beliefs, then this "act as if" can really be seen more like *practice*. You're practicing the behaviors you're going to have anyways as your new perspective really takes hold.

You literally have to create new neural pathways in your brain to teach it to think and feel differently more often. Old habits die hard because you don't really get rid of old habits on a neurological level. Instead, you create an alternative habit that you train yourself to become more comfortable with, and eventually the new habit takes over the old one.

This is why your growth and development is a journey, and one that never really ends. You will always have old patterns and programs that you can potentially fall back into, and you will always have new thoughts and beliefs that you can choose instead. The more you choose empowering thoughts and actions, the more that becomes your default habitual choice. You should also remind yourself of this if you feel like you have to struggle to make the changes you wish to make. You've probably developed certain patterns over a lifetime, and it's going to take time and patience to let them go and replace them with something else. So be gentle with yourself. Making mistakes and screwing up isn't a sign you're doing something wrong, it's a sign you're striving to align yourself to something better – a victory in itself.

The good news is, you can always choose to be OK with wherever you're at right at this moment. The greatest gift of taking responsibility for your experience is that you can always choose to welcome your present circumstance as being a necessary step to getting to where you want to be. You don't ever see babies emotionally beating themselves up and giving up on learning to walk just because they fall down a few times. They instinctively understand there's a process to go through. It's only as adults through conditioning that we're taught to feel bad when we fall down on our journey to something greater.

The questions to ask to bring up ideas for old behaviors to drop and new behaviors to adopt are as follows:

- Would a person who believed (new belief) do this (old behavior)? *Example: Would a person who takes total responsibility for their life complain about their job?*
- What would a person who believed (new belief) do? *Example: What would a person who takes responsibility for their life do? Fix the problem? Find the way it served them? Use it as motivation to help others?*
- Would I rather do (old behavior) and experience (old result) OR do (new behavior) and experience (new result)? *Example: Would I rather complain about this continuing to feel bad without changing anything, OR would I rather take responsibility for the situation, welcome the opportunity it's providing me, and seek a solution to either fix the situation or fix my response to the situation?*

While you can use these questions to shed any old behavior and adopt any new behavior, the three common behaviors that will keep you stuck in any area more than anything else are complaining, blaming, and excuse making. While just about everyone, myself included, will fall into these behaviors from time to time, the key is to look at how much energy is invested into these things and decide if you'd rather save some of that energy for something more constructive – like changing the situation or changing your response to it.

Three Behaviors That Keep You Stuck
Disempowering Behavior 1 - Complaining: Complaining results from focusing *only* on the problem, and what's wrong with how things are. There's nothing bad about noticing things being wrong. This is necessary to make things better. However, complaining is also wasting energy that could be used to actually focus on a solution. A person may have every "right" to complain about something, but it doesn't mean it actually makes the situation any better. If someone says something rude to you in passing, you may be upset about it for a moment, and then let it go. However, if you go around complaining about how rude someone was, you actually just prolong the suffering even if it does feel good to complain temporarily. On top of that, you may reinforce a belief such as "people are rude" and next thing you know, you're upset about how rude people can be just going about your day-to-day business without anything triggering it! Yes, complaining will meet some of your needs (which is why we do it), but it will never truly satisfy you. It's like a drug fix that quickly wears off, and leaves you stuck with the same situation you had before.

Disempowering Behavior 2 - Blaming: While you can't control what others do to you, you always have control of your response to it. Even if other people or circumstances are legitimately at fault for your present circumstance, the only person in this world who has the full power to change your experience is you. If there's no changing your present circumstance, say due to a physical injury, then you can still change your internal response to it which will change your experience. Blaming, like complaining, is a waste of energy *even if you're right.*

Disempowering Behavior 3 - Excuse Making: Excuse making, or justifying your current condition, is really just another form of blaming. It's a way of transferring responsibility from yourself to something else, or even an abstract concept like "time." The way you get yourself stuck is if you say something like "I don't have enough time," then you'll live by that belief and won't see any situations where it's not true. Every excuse you have, just like every belief you have, *is* true because you'll *make it* true.

What kind of alternative behaviors does an empowered person engage in instead? They are, among other things, expressing gratitude, forgiveness, and solution making.

3 Behaviors That Set You Free
Empowering Behavior 1 - Expressing Gratitude: If you believe that within every problem is a solution, then you'll naturally see every problem as an opportunity for growth for which you can be grateful, or at least grateful for an aspect of it. Of course, that doesn't mean it's easy to feel grateful when things are challenging or downright disastrous. Even if you can't feel grateful for the bad things in your life, you probably can feel grateful for the good things in your life – and that's a start. From that point, once you're in a state of gratitude, you can start to shift to how you look at your challenges and see what's to appreciate about them.

Expressions of gratitude starts with an internal feeling of appreciation. Ask yourself, "What am I grateful for? What *should* I be grateful for? *If* there was something to be grateful for, what might it be? What is it about my challenges and problems that I am grateful for?"

The next step is to actually *express* that gratitude outwardly. While simply speaking or writing down what you're grateful for is a good start, it's a much more powerful and different experience to express your gratitude to others.

One thing I highly recommend is to call or write a card to a close family member or friend and tell them how much you appreciate what they've done for you. Be sure to list specific details. Here's another tip, if you're tempted to complain because others haven't expressed their gratitude to you, then the best way to overcome that is to give genuine gratitude to others. Not only will they feel better, but you'll actually receive a rush of endorphins that have been proven to make you happier and improve your health!

Whenever you crave anything, be it appreciation, admiration, or love, ask yourself, how can I give this to others – or even myself? In the act of giving, both parties receive that which is given.

You can also practice this on strangers, especially if they're working at a job in which they're not used to being appreciated for their work.

"You did an amazing job cleaning this table! I want to say thank you for working so hard to make this a great experience here for me."

"You were so helpful and patient with me. I want to tell you how much I appreciate your great service, and that I really admire how great of a listener you are."

You might be surprised at how much you can brighten someone's day by showing them genuine appreciation, but remember that *you* receive an uplift in your emotional state by making someone else feel better.

If you're tempted to complain about something to others, instead, try telling them how you believe this experience *might be* serving you, and why you're grateful for that. Just imagine how different your experience of life would be if every moment you had spent complaining about something was a moment spent being grateful for something.

Another way you can express gratitude would be when someone disagrees or provokes you. What if, instead of getting defensive or offensive, you thanked them? Maybe you don't agree with them, but even saying "thank you for expressing your point of view and giving me something to think about." As long as it's done with sincerity and not in a condescending way, you'll find this not only has the potential to help them drop their guard, but you may find yourself dropping your own guard and realizing maybe they *do* have a legitimate reason for feeling like they do.

Empowering Behavior 2 - Forgiveness: Forgiveness is the empowered person's alternative to blaming. It may be the single most difficult act a person can do, and at the same time the most liberating. If there's one thing that can keep a person stuck for a lifetime, it's holding onto resentment and refusing to forgive. Without forgiveness, a trauma and disempowering message replays over and over on a psychological and emotional level, and this repetition is guaranteed to keep you stuck in some way.

The block to forgiveness usually shows up in the thinking that it means justifying certain actions or behaviors. Forgiveness, however, does not mean condoning wrong doing or even refusing to fight against wrong doing. Rather, it's aimed at releasing your own feelings towards the individual or circumstance, *and that includes forgiving yourself.*

There's a popular quote on forgiveness, which to paraphrase says, "Holding resentment is like drinking poison, and waiting for the other person to die." There's nothing wrong with holding a person responsible for their crimes and taking them prisoner, but not forgiving them by holding onto resentment is essentially taking *yourself* prisoner.

I may ask myself:

- Would I rather hold onto this and feel pain, or would I rather just let it go and be free?
- Is this really worth losing my inner peace over, or would I rather just let it go?
- Why am I able to forgive this person?
- Why am I able to forgive *even more* now?
- Do I want this thing to enslave me with resentment and anger, or do I want the power to choose my own experience to be free?
- If I could forgive, would I?
- Can I let go of needing to be right?

It might not happen right away, but slowly and surely, with enough times of going through this process each day, I can let go of resentment, let go of judgment, and simply be at peace with what is.

For self-forgiveness, look at the times when you've wronged others. If possible, reach out to whomever was wronged and sincerely apologize. If you can make it right, do so. It's not important about whether they forgive you. It's about recognizing your own mistakes, owning up to them, and forgiving yourself. If you can't reach this person, you can visualize the interaction.

The other aspect of forgiveness, that I don't hear talked about as much, is to let go of negative projections onto people, which is a form a judgment. To illustrate the effect of our projections, consider a parent with their child. We assume that they tell them encouraging things like "you're loved," "you're a good person," "you have incredible gifts and talents," that will likely help that child develop those qualities. The parents project certain qualities onto the child, and since children often believe whatever they're told, they'll likely adopt those traits to some degree. This is why it's easy to understand when a child hears negative projections like "You're a bad kid!" "What's wrong with you?" "You can't do anything right, you idiot!" that they'll likely end up with some serious problems down the road.

The difference between a child and an adult is that an adult usually has a better ability to accept or reject incoming projections. If someone calls you an idiot, you may or may not buy into that projection. This doesn't mean the projections of others don't still influence us to some degree (unless we consciously choose to not buy into them). If you've ever been affected by what someone has said to you such as a hurtful insult, you know the power of people's projections to affect you.

If you go around casting negative traits onto others, don't be surprised if some people buy into those traits and live them out in order to prove you right. They don't consciously do this anymore than a child consciously grows up to be a failure because of what a parent or teacher said, but the result is the same – you have the power to influence the behavior of others for better or worse by your own judgments of them.

What this means is that even though you can't control the actions of another, you must still take responsibility for how you *influence* another person. The reason why this is important for breaking through various ruts in your life is because the people in your life will all have a significant, if not the *most* significant, impact on you compared to anything else. If you've ever felt stuck because the people in your life are "keeping" you stuck with their behavior, then you know the importance of managing these relationships. To say you can't change the people in your life is both true and false. It's true in the sense that each person takes responsibility for their own actions, and it's false in the sense that by changing the way you interact with people, you can indeed make a difference in how they react and respond. Studies in numerous areas of psychology all show the powerful degree with which a single person can influence the behavior of many people. This means all change, internal and external, must start from within you.

You're not 100% responsible for another's actions, but you are 100% responsible for your influence on others, and to whatever degree your projections influence another, you must accept your responsibility in that. You are both responsible and *not* responsible for others; to deny either side of this is to only live a half truth.

So how do you respond to someone who genuinely hurts you, or does something they should feel guilty about? In this situation, the natural temptation is to project the pain they've caused you back onto them. That means attacking them and saying something like "How could you do that? You're such an asshole! What's wrong with you?"

The problem with this approach is that you're essentially validating their behavior in a backwards sort of way. By telling them they're a bad person, judging *them* (as opposed to their actions), or in any way insulting them, you're increasing the likelihood they're going to continue on with that behavior even if they do feel ashamed in the short term. Just as a child may feel bad after being told they're stupid and may try harder in school for a short period of time, eventually they may just say "I guess I really am stupid so why change?" after they buy into the projection.

If you really want to have a positive impact on others, you need a positive or empowering projection. Even if you don't care about the well-being of the person who hurt you, at least consider the well-being of all the future people they're going to interact with. Do you want others to experience the same hurt this person caused you? A projection you put onto them may very well be a determining factor as to whether the pain they cause ends with you or continues on to spread to others by their future actions.

A positive projection isn't saying "what you did was ok so don't worry about it." Instead, you want to see that there is good somewhere in that person and speak to that part of them. A better projection would be something like, "I know you're a better person than your actions are demonstrating" "You're a strong person who will overcome this part of you that feels a need to hurt others." "You're really a good person, so what is it that's hurting you that's causing you to hurt others?" "I love you, but what you did really hurt me."

What you say would be dependent on the situation. But the idea is to look for the inner goodness within that person and speak to that part of them rather than their "bad" side. If you don't believe a person has any good in them, but are simply evil, then ask yourself "*if* this person had goodness in them, how would I speak to that part of them?" You want to reinforce the part of others that truly wants to do the right thing, rather than feed into the part of them that caused the pain and wrongdoing in the first place.

While this may be easier said than done in the heat of emotional turmoil, if you do nothing else, then at least avoid attacking them directly. It's fine to oppose their actions, even very strongly. It's fine and even helpful to express how much their actions have hurt you. However, the moment you find yourself tempted to put negative qualities onto them, ask yourself if you really want to be partly responsible for them *continuing* that behavior by you feeding into it.

Another way to handle projections is focusing on your own feelings. This means adopting an approach more like "I hear what you're saying, and what you said (or the way you said it) makes me feel disrespected because…" Or quite simply, "When you say/do that, *I feel*…."

What you're doing here is letting the other person know how you feel without attacking them. You're isolating their actions from them as a person. When taking this approach, you may find that some (not all) people become more willing to hear what you have to say, because they no longer have to defend themselves. A person can't really say you're wrong when you say how you feel, but they can say you're wrong if you project a trait onto them. In other words, saying "I feel bad when you say that because…" is a statement that's hard to argue with. Saying "You are bad when you say that" is a statement that is open to further debate. While some people will be defensive or insist on being right no matter how you do, remember that the only way to break their pattern is to break your *own* pattern of how you respond to them.

The key distinction in all of this is that you want to avoid inducing shame. Shame is a feeling that says "I'm bad." If a person *believes* they're bad, they'll continue to do bad things. This is exactly what research shows, that people who feel shame often end up with addictions, depression, and destructive behavior.

Guilt on the other hand, which is different than shame, is a much more constructive emotion that says "What I DID was bad." People who feel guilt are more likely to correct their actions, because their thought process looks more like this: "I'm a good person, but I did a bad thing. Since good people don't do bad things, I must change my behavior."

Remember that everything about forgiveness and projection also applies to yourself. What kind of projections are you putting onto yourself? Are you insulting and judging yourself?

If so, is it any wonder that you may continue to buy into your own projections? The first step in changing how you treat others is changing how you treat yourself.

Besides cutting out the negative self-projections, you can also instill positive self-projections. This is what affirmations or declarations are. If you've done affirmations and found them to be relatively ineffective, here are some tips to enhancing their effectives.

1. Get your physical body into a high energy state. Jump up and down, listen to inspiring music, and put a smile on your face. This may sound silly, but remember your physical behavior affects your internal mood.
2. Stand in front a mirror and look yourself in the eye.
3. Declare to yourself the positive projection you wish to be true. "I will do this! I am worthy. I am becoming even more successful." Say this with absolute conviction as if you're trying to convince yourself.

Here are some suggestions for affirmation ideas from Jack Canfield: http://jackcanfield.com/affirmations

Finally, remember that your projections have an effect even if they're contained in your own mind. Even mentally projecting negative traits onto another will influence your psyche, and potentially spread outward into your actions and behavior. This is why it's all the more important to be aware of your thoughts and feelings and take conscious control of them.

Empowering Behavior 3 - Solution Making (Empowering Questions): Remembering that all your excuses are true because you'll make them true, the alternative to making excuses (disempowering statements) is to ask yourself empowering questions. Empowering questions lead you to finding solutions rather than simply staying stuck focused on the problem.

Things like "I don't have enough time" becomes "How can I make time?" "What can I do with the time I have?" "Why is this a bigger priority than something else I'm doing?"

"I don't know what to do" becomes "If I did know what to do, what might it be?" "How can I figure out what to do?" "Who might offer guidance that I can talk to?"

Focus on excuses and you'll find limitations, focus on possibilities and you'll find solutions.

I can appreciate that some things will literally be impossible. A person who suffered a terrible injury may not realistically think of a "solution" to how they're going to go outside and play with their kids. The issue here is being attached to only one particular means of reaching an end. Remembering that all you want are your six human needs, ask yourself is there's another way to meet those same needs. A parent who can't play with his kids may have lost one way of getting love/connection with them, but that doesn't mean there aren't alternative means to that same end. The path you take may change, but the destination remains the same.

This means whenever you find yourself going after any particular goal, you'll want to ask yourself *why* you really want that thing. Does a person that wants to be a millionaire really want a million dollars in the bank if they can't spend it? Probably not. They may want to travel, start their own business, drive a nice car. Then they can ask, why do I want those things? Maybe a person wants to travel because it's exciting to learn about different cultures. Maybe they want to travel so they can do charity work. Some people may enjoy it just because it's a break from their routine, and it really doesn't matter as long as it takes them away from their mundane life.

Just keep asking yourself why you want something until you dig down to which of the six human needs it's meeting. Remember, it's probably meeting multiple needs or all of them. Then you can use your empowering questions to ask yourself "how else might I satisfy this need?" until you start to discover alternative paths. It's ok if you don't have "the answer" right away. You may just get one idea, try it out, and that leads you down a path of self-discovery. Soon enough, you may find yourself living a life of far greater fulfillment than you could have ever imagined, even if you *could have* whatever it was you originally desired.

Getting to the bottom of why you really want something will help you overcome "legitimate" excuses because you'll almost always find that there's more than one way to get what you want. This also works for things that aren't really excuses, but more disempowering statements of any sort like "life sucks," "there's no point to it all," "I can't possibly change things." Instead, you can combat these with, "What am I grateful for? What *should* I be grateful for? If I did have something I might be grateful for, what might it be? How can I make something good come out of this? How might the little things I do make a bigger difference than I can currently imagine?"

Step 5: Reinforce A New Perspective Method 2: Change Your Environment

Yogananda says, "environment is stronger than willpower." While much of this book talks about changing yourself from within, both your inner world and outer world are really co-creating each other. What this means is that by changing what you're exposed to, from the people you hang out with, the books you read, the things you watch and listen to, you'll be able to more effectively change your own internal perception. Children are particularly sensitive to adopting whatever perspective they're exposed to growing up which is why we almost always take on certain characteristics of our parents, guardians, grandparents, and extended family.

It may be tempting to think that you're "beyond" being influenced by your environment. While I would always argue you maintain the ability to consciously choose how external influences impact you, that doesn't mean for the vast majority of people it's not going to have at least some impact. This is because our very physiology is built and designed to take in environmental cues to influence our thinking through mirror neurons.

Scientists first discovered mirror neurons when studying how parts of a monkey's brain would light up when performing certain actions. For instance, particular neurons would fire when a monkey picks up a peanut Then they noticed that some of these same neurons would fire in the brain even when the monkey wasn't picking up a peanut, but merely *observing* another monkey picking up a peanut.

What this means is that the brain is recreating the experience in the observer as if the observer was acting out the behavior themselves. Have you ever found yourself experiencing the same emotions that a character is experiencing in a movie? Have you yawned whenever you saw someone else yawn? In terms of more lasting effects, have you ever found yourself taking on expressions and mannerisms of someone you hang out with a lot? If you didn't recreate these experiences in your mind, it would be very difficult to empathize with others and experience the vicarious effect stories have.

These mirror neurons explain a lot about how we pick up behavior and beliefs through observation. A baby doesn't have to be taught how to walk and talk, it just has to observe those around them doing it. If a baby isn't exposed to certain behaviors in their environment, it won't learn them. Just because we grow up and develop a filter through which we can better accept or reject incoming information through our senses, that doesn't mean these mirror neurons aren't constantly working for or against our own growth based on that which we are exposed.

Remembering that environment is (potentially) stronger than willpower, wouldn't it make sense to use what willpower you have to create an environment suited to whatever you're trying to accomplish? If you want to get through whatever rut you're stuck in, and the people in your life are complainers, beat you down for trying to better yourself, and constantly give you bad advice, do you think that environment is serving you or enslaving you?

On the contrary, if you're trying to get out of a rut, and you change your environment to be filled with inspiring stories of people who've gotten through your same struggles and talk about how they did it; if you surround yourself with people at the level where you want to be, and reduce your exposure to naysayers, don't you think that might at least give you a better fighting chance of getting through your challenges?

The energy invested in changing your environment is typically a lot less than it would take to constantly be fighting *against* your environment. It usually amounts to simply making different choices, or as I like to call it, simple substitutions.

For example, when coaching people on improving their diets, one thing I recommend is to get rid of most junk food in the house and replace it with healthier options. While not feasible for every situation, when this is done, it eliminates the constant temptation to snack on something unhealthy. The most important thing to remember about this though is it's not just about getting rid of the bad, but also having some good to replace it, so the person doesn't feel deprived. The only action required, except for perhaps throwing away a lot of food in the kitchen at first, is to pick up one item off a grocery shelf instead of another. In the case of eating out, choosing one restaurant instead of another.

Every choice you make that influences your external environment will also feedback to influence your internal environment. One of the quickest ways to improve your life is by improving your environment.

In almost every case where a person is stuck in any way shape or form, I can usually find an environmental influence. A person feeling discouraged almost always lacks positive encouragement from those in their life while having plenty of people telling them why they're going to fail. A person feeling overwhelmed almost always is exposing themselves to countless ideas without discerning which should be a priority. A person feeling depressed may have people telling them to "cheer up," but lack those who truly understand how emotions work, and who can provide the proper therapy to help them move through their struggles.

Improving your environment boils down to three things; reducing negative influences, reframing negative influences, and increasing positive influences. To do these, you'll use the 3 keys to freedom; awareness of how your environment is influencing you, appreciation of why you've chosen that environment or chosen to stay in it, and action to make a change in either your actual environment or how you perceive your environment.

If you find any of these to be too challenging or unrealistic, remember to ask yourself empowering questions like "how can I do this?" to get your mind focused on solutions rather than problems. While it may be unrealistic to completely overhaul your current environment, it's almost always possible to make small constructive changes that will, when combined with internal reframing of your situation, help you make dramatic changes over time.

Changing Your Environment

To discover the ways your environment may be negatively impacting you, notice any feelings of negativity or limitation in an area where you feel stuck. See if there is anything in your environment that co-exists with that feeling or triggers it. For instance, do you find yourself feeling angry after watching the news? Do you find yourself feeling hopeless about your financial situation after listening to a friend complain about the economy? Do you find yourself feeling unmotivated to exercise after a long drive home after putting in many hours at work?

Here are some questions you can ask yourself:

- *Who* do I spend time with, and *how* do each of these people make me feel? How does each person make me feel about XYZ issue (whatever you're feeling stuck with)? Do the people in my life support my ambitions or not?
- *What* do I watch? What do I read? What do I listen to? How does each of these things make me feel about my challenges? Do they add to my problems or help me solve them?
- *Where* do I spend most of my time? What is my work/home/bedroom environment like? Do these places make

me feel uplifted and inspired, or does they make me feel stressed out?

- *When* do I feel the best, and when do I feel the worst during the day? Are these feelings associated more with a time of day, place, or situation?
- Is there anything in my environment that is holding me back?
- Is there anything in my environment that *I enjoy,* but may actually be keeping me stuck?

The most common sources of environmental influences that keep people stuck in my experience are:

Media – The media, from entertainment to news, is often disempowering *by design.* The news in particular often instills fear, anger, and division among people. While there may be the occasion where a person needs to know what's going on in the world, ask yourself how much news (including celebrity gossip) actually makes a difference in your life? This is a trap I sometimes find myself in. As soon as I ask "what difference does this really make in my life?," I notice that the news quickly loses its interest in favor of things like learning new skills that immediately improve my happiness and productivity. I don't advocate sticking your head in the sand. Understanding what's happening the world has its place, and *can* serve you. However, news can be enslaving when it simply fuels negative emotions, while leaving you deprived of feeling like you have the power to actually change anything. In other words, it's often designed to instill a sense of *"here's what's wrong with the world, and there's nothing you can do about it."* You'll recognize the victims of this when they throw their arms up in the air, complain about the fate of the world, and then go on about their day to day business, changing nothing in their own lives to make things better. In these cases, you'd almost always be better just cutting the news out altogether.

Peers – The saying that you're the sum of the 5 people you spend the most time with reflects the impact our peers have on our lives. Whether it's family, friends, co-workers, or neighbors, these people can all have an influence on you. While you may not have as much ease in controlling who you spend time with (such as co-workers), you should still identify who's having an impact and how. If a person you associate with often complains, for instance, ask "Could I let this person know how their complaining makes me feel?" It's important to lay down boundaries with people about the kind of behavior you will and won't tolerate, so that even if you can't get rid of them, you may be able to persuade them to adjust their actions around you. If you feel this is out of place, you can take a note from one of my mentors who, when he was around co-workers who would make degrading jokes, would simply walk away without saying a word. He gained the respect of his peers because he was seen as a man of integrity, who would not resort to being judgmental towards them, or putting them down for their actions.

Information Overload – In modern times we've become information junkies. Rather than this making things easier, it actually limits our ability to choose effectively. Researchers found that when people were given a choice between 6 jams or 24 jams to purchase, far fewer people purchased when they had 24 options. The reason for this is that the mind gets overwhelmed with so many choices, and it shuts down. We are bombarded with information, sometimes by choice and sometimes by ads, about what we should do in order to be happy, make money, become successful, and improve relationships. With so much information, we're bound to find that a lot of it conflicts. At the very least, there's too much to figure out where to start. This leads to confusion, and confusion leads to inaction by interfering with your ability to discern "what's my next step?" The solution is to filter information to what's most important, learn to find the best sources, and ideally utilize a mentor or coach, who will help you understand that which is most essential at this moment in time.

It's important to understand that what's in your environment isn't inherently good or bad, it just has the *potential* to be good or bad (enslave or serve) depending on your response to it. The idea of reducing negative influences isn't to eliminate them all together, which would be next to impossible, but to manage them so that they don't become overwhelming. The idea of not labeling environmental influences as inherently good or bad also helps you realize that something may be constructive for one person, but could work against another person. It may even be constructive at some times and not others for the same individual.

For instance, exercising at a gym can be beneficial or detrimental for different people. I myself particularly like the convenience of home workouts, but I also recognize that I never seem to get in workouts at home that are as good as those I get in the gym, because my home environment is typically associated with relaxation or business. It seems like my home has too many distractions that take my mind off of training, whereas in the gym, especially seeing others pushing themselves in their workouts, I seem to be better able to stay much more focused on exercise.

For others however, going to a gym may be problematic. They may force themselves to go because they believe it's the only way to get in a good workout, but they find the environment too distracting or intimidating. They may be much more focused at home. This is just one example of how an environment can help or hurt someone depending on the individual, the circumstances, or even just what kind of mood someone's in on a particular day.

The second step to improving your environment is to appreciate why you've chosen something to be in your environment, and see which of the six human needs it meets for you. I understand that you may not have consciously chosen a certain environment, like growing up with family members, or having particular co-workers, but if you continue to allow particular things into your environment, it's because that on some level you believe there to be a benefit to it.

To appreciate how something in your environment is serving you, ask yourself:

- *If* there was a benefit to this thing, what would it be?
- Does this make me feel more certain, excitement, love or connection, significance? Does it help me grow or contribute?

Let's say someone keeps a cluttered environment. To a very neat person, this would be uncomfortable, as they may see cleanliness as a way of gaining certainty. To another person, they may gain certainty by having everything visibly out in the open and within easy reach. The messy person may also feel more certain because by not having to take their time to keep things clean, it saves time to focus on things they consider a bigger priority, which gives them certainty in a more *indirect* way.

When it comes to the things you choose in your environment, one thing to watch out for is confirmation bias. Confirmation bias explains how we seek out people and sources of information that confirm what we already believe – which meets the need for certainty. We like to hang out with people who think and feel the way we do, because it makes us feel more right. This creates a reinforcing system where you believe something, you continually expose yourself to things that confirm your belief, and your belief gets strengthened. This means if someone believes the economy is bad, women/men are crazy, XYZ political party is the cause of all the world's problems, then they'll likely hang out with others who continuously confirm that and it will be very difficult to break this pattern and see things differently.

The deception here is that it often feels *really good* to have people confirm your beliefs, but it may in fact be enslaving you to a limited perspective rather than serving you. The alternative is to choose to hang out with people who not only reinforce positive beliefs, but also remain open to being exposed to new ways of constructive thinking without being overly attached to your own perspective or resistant to an alternative perspective. It's not that you have to buy into an alternative belief, but rather appreciate how it gives you a different perspective on things.

"It is the mark of an educated mind to be able to entertain a thought without accepting it." — Aristotle

Reframing A Negative Environment

Since you'll never be able to eliminate all negative environmental influences, and since even "negative" environmental influences can serve you (like positive ones can potentially enslave you), it's important to manage your perception of these influences so that a "bad" influence will not only *not* bring you down, but can actually be a source of empowerment and strength.

You can adopt many types of mental "frames" to help you take in things from your environment with a different perspective. Sometimes when I feel like people are driving me crazy, I may adopt a slightly humorous perspective that they're helping me learn to be more "Zen." When I worked in customer service and people would act rude or disrespectful, I used it as an opportunity to study human psychology, and to practice my skills of persuasion to see if I could help ease the situation. If I'm stuck in traffic, I may reframe it as an opportunity to catch up on audio books. If something happens that makes me upset, I reframe it as a great opportunity to practice emotional releasing while learning more about myself and what's important to me.

All of these day-to-day experiences, many of which may be unavoidable, can be turned from disempowerments into empowerments that serve you, all by just adopting a new perspective.

Here are some frames you can put on to see things differently:

- This an opportunity to XYZ. *Example: This waiting for my oil to be changed is a great opportunity to mediate or read a book.*
- This is showing me XYZ about myself. *Example: Getting upset over the criticism I received is showing me that I'm attached to other people's opinions of me, and that's something I can work on letting go.*
- This is a game. *Example: I'm going to try to beat my record for how many people I can make smile doing my job today.*

- This is a test. *Example: This setback in my business is a test to see if I'm really committed to my mission.*
- This is helping me become/develop more... *Example: These extremely rude customers are helping me develop more patience and understanding, while developing my skills in negotiation.*
- This is funny because... *Example: My crazy family drama over the holidays will be a really funny story to tell my friends.*

Tips For Creating A Positive Environment

Reducing or eliminating things in your environment that aren't serving you is typically straight forward. While not always easy, it doesn't require much thought and imagination to simply *not* do something. Identifying something more positive and constructive to put in its place, however, requires a certain degree of knowledge and exploration. It can also be tricky because things aren't necessarily inherently good or bad, and this means things that are recommended for one person aren't always recommended for another.

The ability to discern whether something is serving you or not comes with practice, rather than from following any absolute formula. That being said, here are some highly suggested practices from which the majority of people will benefit.

Media

While most mainstream media isn't very uplifting, the good news is that there is an abundance of inspiring books, podcasts, movies, shows, and seminars that can help you in all areas of life. If every month, you read a different book on a subject, in a short time you could be an expert on just about anything.

The way even positive media can enslave you, however, is getting you caught up in an over-abundance of ideas without actual *application*. People get such a high on reading books, going to seminars, and considering all the possibilities for their life that they don't actually apply what they learn – or at least not for very long before jumping onto the next thing.

It's also possible that even media that is meant to educate may have misinformation. This means you should take everything you're exposed to, including this book, with a grain of salt. Explore how it relates to you. Part of our journey is not to get all the answers handed to us on a silver platter, but to have to sift and sort through a variety of materials to not only find answers, but more importantly find what's most important to you. The answers for one person may be different than the answers for another person.

If you'd like to know some of my recommended books and media for a variety of topics, check out the resources section at the back of this book.

Mentors and Coaches

Mentors and coaches are found behind all of the world's most successful people. While I use the word mentor or coach, this could also be a therapist, counselor, trainer, teacher, wise friend, or anyone else in your life that offers you assistance from a place of wisdom. Whether you're working on overcoming an addiction, breaking free of depression, getting yourself in better shape, becoming financially successful, starting a business, getting into or improving a great relationship, or getting over trauma, there's someone who's been where you are and knows the way to break free of the limitations. In the age of the internet, you can often find multiple resources on any topic in an instant.

The quickest way to overcome your obstacles is to learn from someone else who's overcome the same obstacles.

If I knew nothing about a person's challenges and could only offer them one piece of advice to get unstuck, it would be to get a *good* mentor or coach. A good mentor or coach will help bring awareness to your problems, help you appreciate a different point of view, and will be a real-world demonstration of what can be done instead. A coach will help keep you from getting overwhelmed, cut through your BS, and keep you accountable. If they're really good, they will adjust their advice based on your circumstances and personality.

Despite this being the most surefire way to get unstuck, assuming you find a good mentor who knows what they're doing (admittedly not always easy), it's also seems to be something a few people are resistant to. If you suggest to people who are having emotional or relationship problems to seek therapy or counseling, you'll find some people will think they're above that. They'll say their problems aren't bad enough to need outside help, and they'll figure it out themselves.

Pride comes before a fall, because it's pride that will keep you from admitting you need assistance from others – or even a higher power. If you don't think you need a mentor, ask yourself why **all** of the world's top performers from CEOs to athletes to coaches have mentors/coaches (yes, coaches have coaches).

No matter how smart and self-aware you are, we *all* have our blind spots. Mentors, especially when you have more than one, allow you to leverage many more years of wisdom beyond your own. If you have five mentors who average 40 years old, that's an extra 200 years of experience to draw upon to gain different perspective. Mentors also save you the time of having to become a master on every possible topic. If you want to lose a few extra pounds, do you really want to get a degree in physiology to learn how to exercise, or get a degree in psychology to figure out how to stop giving into food cravings? Chances are, you'd rather let the experts handle it.

Despite the fact that we typically have no problem going to a doctor when something is screwed up in our bodies, or a mechanic when something is screwed up with our car, somehow it seems to bypass certain people to go to a guide to improve their happiness.

There are plenty of great resources out there to help you find whatever guidance you need most. If you're interested in my coaching, you can learn more at http://derekdoepker.com/coaching

Accountability

Accountability explains why someone in the military will push themselves beyond their usual limits. It's the same reason a stay-at-home mom will make incredible sacrifices for her children. It's also why a person will work tirelessly at a job they don't enjoy, because they have bills to pay. All of these situations involve our desire to avoid failure when other people are depending on us – or at the very least when other people are *looking* at us.

While mentors or coaches can be a source of accountability, it's not necessary that the people who keep you accountable are people in a position of wisdom. They could simply be a friend, who agrees with you to help each other stay on track with your goals. Two people wanting to lose weight could check in with each other each week to make sure the other is following through with their commitments.

Research has shown that the people most likely to stick with a goal are accountable to others, and suffer the pain of loss if they fail. What this can look like is telling a friend "I'll pay you $20 if I don't submit my resume to 15 places this week." To enhance the effectiveness of accountability, I highly recommend adding a deadline – which is itself a form of accountability to time. If you don't have a person in your life that you can ask to be an accountability partner, a great website that can help you create accountability with is http://stickk.com.

Chapter 10: How The Truth Can Sometimes Keep You Stuck

Between these two statements, which one do you think is true?

1. "Being selfless is good."
2. "Being selfish is good."

The answer is both of these statements are true, and both are false, and *neither* one is true or false, and both are true *and* false.

Confused? That's because you may be used to our typical two-value logic system that says something is either true *or* false. This type of thinking explains why two rational people can be divided on topics, both insisting they're right and anything to the contrary is wrong, and having plenty of proof to back up their point of view.

Four-value logic, on the other hand, encompasses the truth found in a paradox. Paradoxes allow contradictory things to both be true, and in a sense, that makes neither of them true. At first this may make your head hurt, but it resonates with our intuitive understanding that there's almost always a *balance* in things, with any extreme having partial but incomplete truth.

This means staying at *any* type of extreme is typically going to backfire at some point. From that, we get another paradox. Sometimes you *need* to go to the extreme to have balance in the long run. So to even say going to the extreme is "bad" (or good) is both a potentially true *and* false statement. Let's look at some practical examples to help you grasp this.

One thing that seems universally good in our culture is to dress up and look nice. This, under many circumstances, is true. However, do you always want to impress people with your appearance? What if in a certain context you don't want to intimidate people by being all dressed up, but rather need to fit in with the people you're around by being more dressed down? In this context, being too dressed up could backfire and give the impression that you're trying too hard and don't "get" the situation. So to say dressing up, or even just looking your best, is "good" is only true *under a certain context*.

Isn't the importance of balance and understanding context pretty obvious? Yes and no. While the average person will *say* they understand things often work in shades of grey, our actions often reveal we each have biases we can't see past. The reason why they're so hard to see past is because our biases are, in one sense, *correct*. It's just that they're also incorrect too – at least at times. In other words, we typically have adopted things that serve us *most* of the time, but there's almost always going to be situations where these things will go from serving to enslaving us *unless* we have the mindfulness to calibrate our perspective and actions to adapt to each moment.

"All fixed, set patterns are incapable of adaptability or pliability. The truth is outside of all fixed patterns." – Bruce Lee

A designer may believe everything needs to look sleek and professional because that's the world they live, and what their job requires of them. If a design for something like an advertisement is so good it detracts from a message, then it may be counter-productive in that context. There are times where making things downright ugly for the sake of functionality would be beneficial and other times where it would be detrimental.

Making continuous progress and avoiding getting stuck requires constant adaptation and a willingness to adopt different viewpoints depending on the current context you find yourself in. This means a willingness to let go of certain beliefs, or at least to see those beliefs as part of a larger whole. It's not that you're wrong about what you believe, it's just that something may only be true until it's not. Forward progress require a pendulum-like motion that swings back and forth between two extremes constantly, attempting to find balance.

What I'm expressing here is not a rejection of universal principles or laws, but rather a recognition that the way these principles work is in balance and harmony with one another. Taking anything, including principles, in isolation from other principles can be detrimental.

Even proven principles of success can enslave you when practiced out of harmony and balance with other principles.

Take for instance the importance of service to others. Service through creating value in the world is the key to abundance – be it financial or emotional. However, if a person serves others at the exclusion of serving themselves, they'll starve to death before they get a chance to help as many people as they would like. The most tempting excuses are where you can say "What I did was good and right," and be telling the truth. When you do what's right, *but omit another essential element*, it's *not* doing things right. It's sort of like walking around without pants on talking about how great it is that you put a shirt on.

The truths we tell ourselves can get us stuck more readily than the lies we tell ourselves. I'm not saying that truth will always enslave you. Only that, like anything else, it can enslave or serve you – and in this case, it's based on whether or not it's the *whole* truth. Something that is 99% true and 1% lie is a dangerous deception, because it has the weight of truth to make you buy into it.

Half-truths will keep you stuck just as easily as whole lies.

Here are some common pieces of paradoxical advice you may have heard from well-meaning people about what it takes to improve your life. While I'll attempt to "resolve" the paradox, remember that you can't ever really resolve a paradox. They remain open to never-ending contemplation. While I provide my own perspectives and some insights learned from wise mentors, the beauty of all of this is that the paradoxes have a "charge" to them similar to a positive and negative terminal of a battery. There is a constant flow of energy between the positive and negative terminals, and this dynamic flow is what moves you forward in life. When you cut off this flow and sit on one extreme or the other, you get stuck.

Common Paradoxes and Opposing Forces
Selfish Vs. Selfless
To some degree, survival requires an element of looking out for your own needs above and beyond the needs of others. Since you're the only person that you have total control over, it makes a lot more sense to invest your energy into where you have the greatest impact – your own life.

On the other hand, while survival of the fittest is debatably said to be the way of things in nature, it can also be said that human beings rule this planet because we've transcended our animal instincts. We've learned to work together, and use our consciousness to bypass selfish instincts. Even certain non-human animals work together and look out for each other in tribes and pacts for their survival. Our entire civilization is built upon cooperative effort and the ability for people to develop specialized skills that require interdependence on one another.

These seemingly contrary instincts show up in our needs for love/connection vs. significance. We need to feel connected to one another because, in addition to other reasons, we know that on our own we don't stand as much of a chance for survival. However, we also want to feel special and unique, as that gives us a feeling that we have a place in the world and can't just be replaced by anyone else.

This paradox also shows up in the understanding that while we are responsible for our own actions and each person must make their own decisions, we are *also* responsible to others – but they still must accept responsibility for their actions just like you must accept total responsibility for your actions. Remember that a paradox can't be logically understood with our two value logic system, so let's look at symbolism to help understand this.

A farmer is responsible for his crops in that he must plant them, water them, nourish them, and prevent animals from eating them. A farmer can't sit back and hope that the crops grow and sow themselves. At the same time, a farmer isn't responsible to the degree in which there may be drought or natural circumstances that prevent his crops from growing. So to the degree in which he can impact the growth of the crops, he's responsible. To the degree in which it's beyond his control, he's not.

This is pretty easy to understand, and something we can readily accept. In our lives as metaphorical farmers, our words and actions become like seeds that we plant in the world. These can be encouraging words and positive influence (crops), or they can be discouraging words and actions that negatively impact others (weeds). If a farmer plants a bunch of weeds along with his crops, he can't complain that they've overtaken his field. If a farmer fails to plant any seeds, he can't complain when the field doesn't produce. This explains our responsibility to others, especially to those that literally depend on us, as in a parent-child relationship. Another way of putting this is that whether you like it or not, you *will* impact others by your mere presence on this planet. You can't avoid responsibility to others whether you want to or not.

Where *personal* responsibility comes into play is that the farmer can't even plant seeds and sow the field if he/she hasn't taken care of themselves. If the farmer doesn't eat, get enough sleep, and learn the skills of farming, then all his good intentions to plant a great field will be wasted when he ends up too sick and malnourished to even go into the field. So if a farmer wishes to produce something of value, he can't do so at the expense of taking care of themselves. In other words, you can't feed the hungry if you starve to death.

In general, men tend to naturally prioritize themselves above others and taken to an extreme, this can lead to not caring enough for those closest to them. Women, in general, often tend to prioritize others above themselves, due to the feminine tendency to prioritize love/connection over significance, and may neglect their own needs to both their detriment and the detriment of the very people they want to care for.

The balance I've learned from my greatest mentor, Brandon Broadwater, is to focus first on yourself, then spread out from there to your spouse/partner, family and friends, and then the world at large. Taking care of yourself *doesn't* exclude you from having a responsibility to others. Your responsibility to others doesn't supersede or even equal that of your responsibility to care for yourself. There must be a constant balancing act, making what's best to do at one moment not the best thing to do at another moment.

Sometimes the ego says you have to build yourself up (significance) so that others like you, which leads to what we typically call "egotistical" behavior. Our ego *doesn't* just use acts of selfishness to serve itself. The ego can go the other way and say you have to do everything for everyone else so that others like you. People who give all of themselves to others and end up destroying their own lives in the process are not in a state of true love and service. This is just the other side of the same ego coin. In other words, one is doing things for others only because they still want something for *themselves* – approval (connection).

Selfless acts, done *at the expense of one's greater priorities,* can be just as egotistical and destructive as selfish acts.

Either extreme can potentially destroy you and those around you. The path to freedom is to let go of the whole thing by finding a state of not being overly attached or resistant to people approving of you, but rather coming from a place where you serve yourself and others from the motivation of love.

True love may result in *short-term* sacrifice, but almost always maintains a balance that allows you to meet your *long-term* needs. It always takes into account the bigger picture. We can't readily look at a single action and judge it as constructive or destructive without seeing a bigger picture. Giving all your food away to someone who needs it more can be a great act of love. It can also be a very "selfish" and destructive act if a person has done this every day for the past month, resulting in the death of him and his family by starvation. While this makes obvious sense when taken to an extreme like starving to death, where we tend to miss this is in all the little things we sacrifice from our long-term needs, like our financial stability or emotional welfare, in an attempt to please others.

Wanting approval comes from the ego, and this want can be met with both selfish and selfless acts. True service to others and yourself results when you no longer act out of ego-based wants, but act out of love.

Questions I've found helpful are "can I let go of wanting to please others?" "Would I rather give my power to feel good about myself to others or keep it for myself?" Once I've found myself no longer trying to just please people, but acting from a state of emotional neutrality and rationality, then the right course of action is usually clear. It also helps to ask, "How does this affect things in the long-run?" Short-term sacrifices are fine, and essential at times. If those sacrifices are setting you down a path of excessive loss in the long-term, however, then they can be harmful to *everyone* involved, no matter how good your intentions are.

Change Is Bad Vs. Change Is Good
Change, and particularly changing oneself, is a highly charged topic. Some people have an aversion to changing themselves. After all, shouldn't we love and accept ourselves just as we are? You should just "be yourself." Isn't the whole problem that we're telling ourselves, that there's something wrong with us and that is, in itself, what's creating the problem? If we stopped projecting flaws onto ourselves like we stop projecting flaws onto others, wouldn't that really be the fix to the problem?

The other school of thought is that change is good. You don't really think you are perfect, do you? If your life isn't where you want it to be, the way to make it better is to change things – and all change starts from within. This means changing yourself is not only good, but essential to getting what you want out of life.

The paradox is yes, you should love and accept yourself as you are and no, you shouldn't want to change what's here right now, AND you should also want to change yourself and love and accept those changes.

Confused? Here's an analogy to help. An oak tree shouldn't want to ever be an apple tree or feel bad that it's anything other than an oak tree. An oak tree is perfect as it is just like an apple tree is perfect as it is. However, while an oak tree will always *fundamentally* stay the same, it will also constantly be changing. In a year, that oak tree may have grown, shed some leaves and grown some new ones, have a few branches broken and new ones that have taken its place, and undergone this daily process of change that happens to all things in nature.

In your life, whether you like it or not, you are *constantly* changing. These changes are physical, psychological, and emotional. Some changes are so gradual you may not notice them for many years, but it's absolutely impossible to move through life being exactly the same from day to day – or even moment to moment.

So to say "I don't want to change, I like myself just as I am" is to deny a very principle of nature that *nothing* stays the same. You don't plant a tree in good soil and water it because you want to change what type of tree it is, you nourish it so it grows to its fullest potential. The difference between you and a tree however is that you can *choose* whether or not to nourish yourself – and therefore your growth or decay is up to you. You have the choice as to whether or not you're going to grow (and therefore change) to become your fullest potential.

You don't have a choice in the matter of whether or not you want to change. The question is whether or not you want to leave that change up to chance or choice.

Just to balance the paradox, you should also be OK with wherever you're at now. This acceptance doesn't mean resignation to staying this way forever. You can accept something in the present moment while working to change it, so that it's not there in the future – such as accepting you have a bad habit and then correcting it. This acceptance is more of an acknowledgment that you're always at some point in the journey of development and won't ever be perfect. You're always going to have issues you're working on, and that's part of the excitement of life. Remember, *you have an emotional need for growth*. Without anything to work on in yourself, you have no way to grow. In this respect, your flaws actually serve to help you learn and grow, in addition to helping you be more compassionate towards other people's flaws.

The way to be in the present moment and oriented towards the future is to ask yourself questions like:

- Who am I *becoming*?
- What is this moment leading to?
- What direction am I going in – growth or decay?
- Am I using my situation to enslave me or empower me?
- What kind of path are my current actions leading me down?

Emotions Vs. Logic

Where some people get stuck is when they pit their gut against their brain. You may have heard to listen to your gut and follow your heart, but you may also hear that you should "use your head" and think rationally. So which is it?

The first thing I want to point out is that intuition isn't always the same as an emotional response. Intuition may speak to you through emotions, but that doesn't mean all of your emotions/gut feelings are your intuition. Your biases and fears can also speak to you through emotions and feelings. A person with a racial bias may have a bad feeling when seeing a person of a certain race and feel like he's in danger, but this can be a programmed bias that isn't necessarily a sign that there is genuine danger.

Intuition can be a very helpful guidance system that often *uses* logic rather than defies it. Your mind can process a lot of information subconsciously that you're not directly aware of, and then use your emotions to give you its findings.

For instance, a person may get a feeling someone is lying to him and he doesn't know why. What could be happening is that the subconscious mind is picking up on many different body language cues and processing them as signs of deception. The result is a gut feeling that he's being deceived. While all of that is happening, the conscious mind, unable to pick up on all these subtle things, isn't able to readily ascribe a reasoning to why he has that gut feeling. There is a logic behind the intuition although you may not be aware of it. In this case, it feels like a purely emotional response, but there are rational reasons for feeling that way. This does *not* mean however that your intuition is always right, just that it can have a higher probabillty of being right.

How do you differentiate between "true" intuition and everyday emotions? This takes awareness and practice, practice, practice. The simplest technique I've learned comes from emotional releasing which you can learn about from books like The Sedona Method. It requires letting go of your attachment and resistance to feelings. When you let go of your emotional attachments and just be OK with what is, you'll find that your biases drop away, and your intuition may actually get stronger and clearer. This can help you discern between genuine threats or opportunities vs. perceived threats and opportunities.

My personal "bias" is in favor of not having a bias with either one of these things. I believe people should learn to develop their rationality using exercises and thought processes, and be open to letting go of their emotional attachments. At the same time, I believe we developed emotions for a good reason and shouldn't neglect them in favor of pure rationality, which can – at times – lead to an undesirable courses of action. I believe the more you embrace and appreciate both of these things for the role they play without getting deceived by biased emotions *or* logic, the more you'll find they work in conjunction with one another rather than against each other.

If you want to understand a more functional way of looking at the value of intuition, Malcom Gladwell's book Blink points out that our intuitive process tends to be more reliable when making big life decisions that have too many factors for our limited conscious mind to weigh. More straightforward problems are often easily resolved using rational thinking.

Positive Thinking Vs. Negative Thinking

One of the big myths in the self-help world is that it's all about thinking positively. This ironically tends to lead people to beat themselves up whenever they don't have positive thoughts, or stress themselves out about being stressed out. The isolation of positive from negative also leads to sticking one's head in the sand and ignoring very real problems that need to be addressed in one's life and the world in general.

On the other extreme, pessimists and cynics may say they have a more realistic perspective on the world, but then they may lack hope, and fail to find solutions. They focus so much on the problems that they aren't able to appreciate the opportunity that exists within every challenge. As covered quite a bit in this book, appreciation means appreciating the positive *and* negative, welcoming and accepting what is, and dropping judgment towards either extreme.

The balanced approach tends to lead to conscientious behavior which is the characteristic most associated with long life span. A conscientious person is both able to identify problems and also identify solutions. They don't purposely blind themselves to positive or negative things, but make themselves aware of everything so they can take the best course of action.

I don't go around in constant fear that I'm going to get in a car accident. At the same time, I also have an emergency kit in my car because I realize that getting in a car accident, or even just getting stranded somewhere, is a real possibility. You can recognize bad things that can and will happen, but rather than invest your energy into worry, you invest it into fixing or preventing it. If you can't fix it, you can work on fixing your response to it.

"If your problem has solution, then why to worry about it? If your problem doesn't have solution, then why worry about it?" – Chinese Proverb

Remember, pain is a powerful motivator and signal to create awareness. If you refuse to face what is causing you pain, it's like living on painkillers and not knowing that something is wrong in your body, until it leads to serious injury or death. Another danger of ignoring the negative and only focusing on the positive is it reduces your ability to empathize with others. How annoying is it when you're really struggling, and someone can't appreciate what you're going through because they're too cheery?

The most balanced approach comes when you can let go of labeling everything as good or bad and see it as "empowering" or "disempowering" *based on your choice.* That means you get to decide what you make of your experience. This doesn't mean it's always fun or enjoyable. Many of the most transformative things are incredibly painful, but at least you have the ability to let something serve you to create a brighter future should you decide you want it to.

Work Hard Vs. Work Smart

People who work hard love to wear it as a badge of honor. They'll complain about people who take the easy way out. How many lazy people do you know who are living their dreams? Those who work smart may believe hard work is for suckers. Human beings don't rule this planet because we're the most physically capable, but rather because we're the most mentally capable. Ingenuity is behind all the great leaders and business owners. CEOs and decision makers are typically among the highest-paid people.

So do you work hard or do you work smart to get to where you want to be? The obvious answer is – it depends. As James Malinchak says, "it's not about working harder or smarter, it's about working right." In some cases, this means putting your nose to the grindstone and getting things done through sheer hard work. In other cases, it may mean leveraging the skills and abilities of others so that things are done efficiently with synergy rather than excess effort. Still, in other cases, getting the job done may simply mean making one small change in your approach that requires zero extra energy, or may even save you energy.

Something people often ask me when wanting to know about getting in shape is "what's more important, diet or exercise?" They may ask something like, "what's the easiest way to get rid of belly fat if I can only do *one* thing?" What these people are trying to do is not necessarily take the easy way out, but seek efficiency. They want to know how to prioritize their decisions given a limited about of time, energy, and willpower. *Sometimes* focusing on the 20% that's going to give you 80% of your results is a good thing, and other times, you either do it *right* or you don't do it at all.

When I hear people asking me about diet vs. exercise for health, I'm tempted to ask them whether they think their brain or their heart is more important for life. While you could debate about the relative merit of each, at the end of the day thinking in terms of what's necessary for the job is all that matters.

There will be times where getting to where you want to go takes intelligence (your own or others), times where it takes sheer effort (your own or others), and times where it takes doing absolutely nothing when tempted to do something that will yield you the results you want. There will also be times where what worked one day won't work the next. Forget about what's hard, easy, smart, dumb, convenient, typical, or anything else, and focus on what's *right* for *right now*.

Copy Vs. Create

For anyone involved in creative endeavors, or even just trying to figure out creative solutions to your problems, you'll likely run into this issue – do you simply copy what's been proven to work, or do you create your own solution?

On one hand, it makes sense not to reinvent the wheel. If someone else has figured out a solution to your problem, you can save yourself a lot of headache. This is why having a mentor is so important. At the very least, it makes sense to read a book or attend a seminar to learn more about the areas in which you lack knowledge and insight.

On the other hand, it may seem disingenuous to just copy what everyone else does. A copy-cat business won't be successful. Speaking to people from scripts rather than from the heart can prevent a genuine connection and presence. A person that's unoriginal in what they do will quickly blend into the crowd and fail to stand apart.

This even plays out when asking for advice. While someone may offer great advice about worked for them, can you really say your situation is exactly the same? Even if we appreciate the insights of others because we don't have to figure it out ourselves, it can feel at times that someone else can't possibly know what's best for us because they're not us and they haven't lived in our shoes.

In my marketing training, I teach a simple formula that resolves these two extremes. It's my formula for innovation which I believe is the sweet spot in the middle of these two polarities. Even if you're not building a business, this formula works for coming up with innovative solutions to any of your problems – be it in your health, relationships, or overall happiness.

Imitation + Creation = Innovation

This formula comes from my observation that the most successful people tend to both copy what works, while at the same time adding something new to the mix. In other words, they take something that's been done before and make it their own.

Of course, there are times where strict imitation is the best approach. This could be when first learning a new skill where you won't have the perspective to add your own twist. There are also many times where something is so fundamental and principle-based, that making any changes to it would only lead to disaster.

There are other times where pure creation is the best approach. This is best when a problem can't be solved within an old paradigm. Whether you look at it as outside-the-box thinking, or just getting into a brand new box all together, the overall idea is that there will be times where you have to come up with something that's never been done before to solve a problem.

Another way to look at these two extremes is in the leader/follower model. While we're taught that being a leader is "better" than being a follower, in actuality, it takes being a good follower to be a good leader. All great leaders had their role models and those they got advice from while in positions of leadership.

Like all the paradoxes, there's usually a mix of both, and a time and place for each. The danger is in thinking someone else will be able to tell you the exact blend that you need for your situation. This is why you must balance this concept with the other things you've learned – like taking action to gain perspective. Sometimes you'll only discover the answers by testing things out and seeing what works. This means a willingness to accept failure and mistakes by appreciating how they're helping you in finding a balanced approach.

Finding The Paradox

While these examples are some of the common paradoxes I've seen, many "truths" contain a paradoxical element or balancing factor that needs to be accounted for. Any strongly held belief, even if it's helpful or accurate, can keep you stuck if you haven't found the other truths that work in conjunction with it.

It's important when looking at your own beliefs or anything you've been told, to run them through your own inner "truth filter." You shouldn't believe everything you're told, not even by me. Not only can I (or anybody else, for that matter) be genuinely mistaken, but people can only share from their perspective and experience. That means there will almost always be some degree of bias, even if that's just the way language is limited in its ability to convey concepts.

As a coach, one of my main jobs is to identify people's stumbling blocks and give them advice that is tailored to them. For some people, I may recommend they increase their discipline by setting deadlines, getting accountability, and having clearly defined goals. Other people may need the exact opposite approach, by adopting a more flexible go-with-the-flow type mentality. They could be encouraged to ditch their routines and to-do lists and instead adopt the skills in following where their intuition leads them.

Neither approach is inherently right or wrong. Each has its place, and you must learn to discern for yourself the areas in which you may be more biased in favor of one approach rather than another. Otherwise, when all you have is a hammer, everything will seem like a nail.

Here are a number of questions you can ask yourself when looking at any belief you have, statement you've heard, or viewpoint you see:

- Is this true for me?
- Is this the whole truth?
- Is this true for everyone? Is there anyone for whom this may not be true?
- Is this true right now?
- Was there ever a time where it wasn't true? Will there be a time when it's not true?
- When is this true?
- When is this false?
- Does this require something else to maintain balance?
- How is this neither true nor false?
- How is this both true and false?

What you'll often find when doing this, is that many beliefs and viewpoints you have, even if they're "true," may not contain the whole truth. Something that is true for you at some point may not always be true. If this is the case, consider what other elements you feel may help bring about a balanced perspective, and remember that often the right thing to do is more about doing something at the right time.

Chapter 11: The Secret To Overcoming Fears Of Failure

Fear of failure is one of the most common things that keeps people stuck. We've been conditioned to believe that being wrong or making a mistake is a bad thing. In school, we get a big red X on a paper every time we make a mistake. On the contrary, we get rewarded for repeating what we've been told is the truth, even though much of what you learned may later prove to be inaccurate. On a subconscious level, that makes us believe being right is more important than exploration and learning. So we go off into the world as adults with an attachment to being right, and a fear of being wrong, rather than a desire to learn and grow.

When you truly understand just how significant this is, you'll come to realize that not only are many of your problems stemming from this conditioning, but many of the world's problems of fighting, disharmony, and lack of compromise stem from our condition of needing to be right. If you can't ever say "I could be wrong," and be OK with it, then you *will* get stuck in some area.

Our desire to be right, while often reinforced by external programming, is really just an over-emphasis on our need for certainty. To be more specific, it's often from a desire to control everything in our world, including circumstances and other people. Since this type of absolute certainty is never going to be possible, you must learn to let go of an attachment to it if you want to push through your fear of failure.

There are several ways you can overcome this attachment to certainty:

1. Gain *inner* certainty/confidence
2. Welcome uncertainty
3. Let go/Non-attachment

Gaining Inner Certainty/Confidence

It's been my observation that the more one has a sense of certainty in themselves, their ability to handle whatever comes their way, and faith, the more they can handle the inevitable uncertainty they're going to face. They feel less compelled to try to control others and themselves and simply go with the flow. This inner certainty is the type of confidence that is bred from real-world experience and success rather than a false, ego type of bravado.

Certainty Building Tactic 1: Success Focus

The difference between confident and unconfident people typically isn't a matter of confident people somehow being born better or having never failed. Most of the time they just *choose* to remember their successes rather than their failures, or see their failures as ways they learned to be better. This is a conscious choice anyone can make, but since we're more motivated by pain than pleasure, the mind will naturally default to thinking about past failures rather than past successes. You must consciously choose to think differently.

The first way you can start to build your confidence is by asking yourself, "When have I been successful in the past?" Make a list of some of your life's biggest accomplishments. If you're struggling with a particular challenge in your life, consider other times you've gone through something similar and came out OK, or even thrived. At the moment of facing fear, it also helps to recall a time where you've faced your fears and pushed through successfully.

What we naturally tend to do is ask ourselves "What if ABC bad things happens?" when facing uncertainty. However, you can just as easily ask yourself "What if XYZ good thing happens?" by recalling positive experiences from your past. We create our future expectations based on previous experience, and previous negative experiences tend to be more readily recalled than previous positive experiences. By consciously shifting your focus, you can develop a stronger sense of confidence by remembering that you have just as many (or more) successes as you do failures.

Certainty Building Tactic 2: Mentors and Support

Mentors and outside support isn't just helpful, but *required* at times to get past sticking points. There will be times where you ask "what's my next step?" and don't have an answer. While I believe we have many of the answers within ourselves, we also all have our own blind spots. There will also be times when you just don't have the technical knowledge to know how to proceed with something, requiring you to get a mentor or other resources to aid you. All the world's top performers, from CEOs to athletes to self-help gurus, have mentors and outside support.

Finding a knowledgeable mentor for assistance will let you leverage *their certainty*. It's much easier to move forward not knowing all the answers when you know you'll have people you can turn to in order to help you get through the periods of uncertainty.

Welcome Uncertainty

The key to becoming more accepting of uncertainty is to remember that it is not just an inevitability, but it's actually a part of what makes life *exciting*. If the outcomes you wanted were guaranteed, this would actually get pretty boring after a while. It's like knowing the spoilers to every movie, TV show, or book. Besides the boredom factor, there's a lot to be learned through having to go through periods of uncertainty. The process of being curious and discovering answers about the unknown is one of the most fulfilling things you can experience.

A psychological trick to changing feelings about something is to "reframe" what you're telling yourself about the situation. Things like fear, confusion, and uncertainty can all be reframed to more empowering states like excitement and curiosity.

Instead of saying "I don't know what will happen, *and that's scary*," you can tell yourself a different story. "I don't know what's going to happen *and I can't wait to find out*" would be a simple way to turn that fear into excitement. "I wonder what will happen when I move forward with this?" is a way to turn that uncertainty into curiosity. Finally, ask yourself questions like "Can I welcome the excitement this will bring me?" and "Why am I so excited by this?"

Another important thing to do to welcome uncertainty is to look to your past failures and see how they have actually benefited you. Where have you screwed things up, and either been OK or even turned out better for it? What are the mistakes you've made that you're grateful for? How has past failure been necessary for your current success? If you feel like a particular failure or unwanted event hasn't served you, ask yourself "*If* there was a lesson there, what would it be?" When you start to appreciate that your failures have served you as much or more than your successes, the negative charge around making a mistake starts to diminish.

Non-Attachment

The ability to remain unattached to *how (and even if)* you'll reach an outcome is particularly important to overcoming the fear of failure. Sometimes we get so focused on doing things a certain way or having a particular outcome that we become blinded to all the other possibilities that exist that may be even better. When you realize that there's probably a much better way of reaching an outcome than whatever you *think* you need to do, you'll be more open to screwing things up and learning better alternatives. The less attached you are to a certain way of doing things, and that includes saying "I need to do XYZ to be happy in life," the more open you become to all the possibilities that really exist beyond your current level of awareness.

This unattached state is more childlike, in that a child simply explores and experiments with things just to see what happens. They're in constant awe at what they experience in each moment, without constant judgment or labeling things as success or failure. Imagine your life if you just tried things for the hell of it without worrying about success or failure. What new things might you discover? How much easier would it be if you approached whatever you're fearing as a game or experiment, instead of something that's going to make or break your happiness? While it's easier said than done to remain in this state of non-attachment, as you strive to maintain this frame, you'll find it easier and easier to adopt.

This also means having the ability to let go of goals that no longer serve you. Much of my success has come from being a very good quitter, while also being a very good learner. Several years ago I set the intention to become financially free so I could quit my job to work in my own business. This first led me to real estate, where I followed the courses, networked with local real estate investors, and learned a lot about business in general. Eventually I found it wasn't really my calling, and moved on to starting an online business. This began with blogging, writing articles, and eventually to my success in publishing books.

Looking back, even in the areas where I didn't have any outward success, I was still successful in learning new skills and discovering things about myself. In a certain respect, *every single one* of these endeavors brought me financial freedom, but not because they made me enough money to quit my job. Instead, they each taught me what I would later need to know when I found my current calling, publishing books and coaching.

"A good traveler has no fixed plans and is not intent on arriving." - Lao Tzu

While it could be argued that if I had just stuck with anything long enough I would have succeed, I'm happy I listened to my intuition when it told me I was ready to let go of what I was doing and move onto the next thing. We've been brainwashed into thinking quitting is a bad thing. While perseverance is necessary for success in all areas of life, paradoxically, so is quitting – so long as you're quitting on the right thing at the right time.

How do we resolve the idea that you need to persevere, but also quit? You've probably heard how Thomas Edison had over 1,000 failed attempts to build a light bulb, and we're all grateful for his perseverance. Of course, he didn't repeat the same method to building that light bulb. He quit the methods that didn't work, in order to try something new. In other words, he kept the overall goal the same, but quit when a certain method of reaching that goal didn't work.

Quit on the details, not the destination.

This can mean quitting a workout program that's no longer getting results, quitting a job that's no longer fulfilling, or quitting interacting with people in a way that's leading to disharmony. No matter how great something may have worked in the past, anything that served you at one point in time can enslave you at another point in time. Flexibility and adaptability is the key to staying unstuck.

What set you free yesterday can enslave you today. What enslaved you yesterday can set you free today. Right action requires right timing.

When considering whether or not to persevere with something, some things to consider are:

- **Is this something to be practiced?** Any particular skill will require practice to become proficient. Sometimes people give up because something "isn't working," when actually they just haven't put in the necessary time and practice to make it work. It's also important to recognize that when developing any skill, there will be a plateau point after a period of rapid progress. This doesn't mean you're stuck, just that your next breakthrough can take a while. You may even experience a decline in performance before your next breakthrough.
- **Does this resonate with me?** Some people will live their whole lives going after goals that aren't really their own. Their parents, friends, or culture instills in them the sense that they "should" be doing something, but if they took an honest look at their own desires, they may find they're just living out someone else's dream. Ask yourself, is what you want really what *you* want? This also includes taking time to actually consider *why* you want something. A person may say they want a great romantic relationship, but what he *really* may want is to feel loved. Are there other ways to feel loved that don't require being in a particular kind of relationship? Another person may

want a certain job, but then realize she really just wants the financial income that job provides. Ask "why do I want this," and see where your intuition leads you.

- **Is there another way to accomplish this?** No matter what you're going after, there are going to be a number of ways to get it. If you find yourself stuck on any one approach that you can't seem to make work, consider a new tactic. Sometimes, just taking a break and coming back to what you were doing later is enough to make a breakthrough. This is something you can consider after you've given something an honest effort – not an excuse to jump from one thing to the next.

Chapter 12: Why Good Intentions Are Not Enough

There's a harsh truth that gets a lot of people who read books like this stuck. That truth is that you can mean well, think well, have a heart of gold, and even act on what you believe is best, but that's not enough to get you where you want to be. All of the advice offered by most self-help books id great for getting you inspired to take your life in a better direction, but none of it will matter if you don't have the actual *practical skills* to change things.

If you take your car to a mechanic, you probably want them to be honest and ethical, right? You also probably want them to work on your car and do the job. I'm also willing to bet that you want them to be a *good* mechanic - meaning they can get the job done and *do it well*. Let's just say the mechanic couldn't actually fix your car, but they are a "really nice person" and "really tried their best." Is this someone you want working on your car?

This is plainly obvious when thinking about jobs, but how often do we stop to look at our own lives and see the areas where we need certain skills that we're lacking? This can be especially common in relationships. Two people really care about each other and want to make the most of the relationship, and yet things still fall apart. Why is this? Because they lacked certain skills like communication techniques, understanding the other person's psychology, and being an effective listener just to name a few. All the good intentions in the world won't fix lacking the right education and the practice necessary to pro-actively *make things work*.

Another common situation I've found that keeps people stuck is they *do* have skills, but they rest on those skills and think they don't need to develop them further or develop complementary skills. I struggled with this for a long time, because I wanted to build a business around my extensive knowledge of health and fitness. However, it wasn't enough to just have skills in the area of fitness, I also needed to learn how to market myself, network with people, and develop the ability to convey my message effectively.

It's very easy to get caught up in the mindset that "I've done enough work, can't I just sit back and stop developing myself?" In the short term, the answer is yes, you can get away with that for a while. In the long term however, failure to continue to develop your skills and abilities and gain new ones *will* get you stuck.

There's a skill to conquer any challenge and resources to learn any skill. Ongoing struggles become a choice when you choose not to learn.

This means asking yourself things like:

- How can I become the type of person that has XYZ? *Example: How can I become the type of person that has great relationships?*
- What can I learn to improve this situation? *Example: What can I learn to increase my chances of getting a promotion?*
- Who can I learn from who has conquered this challenge? *Example: Who can I learn from who has lost a lot of weight while caring for 3 children and working a full time job?*
- What skill am I lacking that, if I learned, would help me overcome this challenge?
- What can I do to *practice* this skill and get feedback? *Example: What can I do to practice my communication skills and hear from others how well I'm doing?*

It's also important to recognize when learning a particular skill *isn't* necessary, and instead you're much better off getting the assistance of someone else. If you wanted your own website, do you need to learn everything about web design, or would it make a lot more sense to hire someone? And even if you can't afford it, remember that there are countless broke college students who are willing to do things for their portfolio. It's also possible that you have skills you can trade for someone else's skill. Even in these situations where you find you don't need to learn the skill yourself, you may find that other skills like communication, negotiation, and management can be essential. So learning and developing skills never stops being a priority.

The thing to remember is, like most everything else, this is a step-by-step process. Some people say, "I need to learn how to create my own business, but it's too expensive to hire a mentor or attend a seminar on the subject." When something is too big to take on right now, you must break it down into smaller, more manageable, more readily doable things you can tackle.

I would ask myself things like:

- Is there something I can learn right now to get me started?
- Is there a skill I can learn to increase my finances so that I can get the training I need?
- Is there another way to reach my goal?
- What can I do in the meantime to keep me moving forward?

When I decided to start my own business, I was dead broke and living paycheck to paycheck. I wanted to launch a fitness guide, but there were a lot of startup costs that made it impossible for me to get the training and resources I needed. Instead of using that as an excuse to give up, I broke it down into tiny actions that I could take towards my goal. I volunteered at seminars to get free training. I read books and signed up for free courses on marketing. I started making a few extra bucks teaching guitar lessons to raise capital. I eventually found self-publishing books to be a way to make some income without needing a lot of money to invest up front. I was always on the lookout for whatever my next "target" that I could hit which would keep me moving forward. I didn't have to see how it would all fit together, I just kept needed to keep going and learning whatever I could. Eventually, I knew I would find the ways to get the resources like money and education that I needed. In the end, I succeeded.

This meant that I had to have the willingness to hustle and do whatever it took to *make* a way to what I wanted. This mentality seems to be lost on a number of people, and it's the reason why they find themselves stuck. They only see one single, impossible way out of their circumstance, instead of seeing the countless little things they can do to *create* a new circumstance.

If the path to what you want is blocked, make a new path.

A single act can carry a lot more weight than its direct outcome, in that it can be the determining factor in what course you set yourself on. Research done on integrity shows that just one little lie often leads to making subsequent lies far easier to justify. Likewise, one honest act tends to reinforce future honest behavior.

This happens in many areas of life. A person cheats on their diet one meal, so they decide it's not so bad to cheat for the rest of the day, then they figure they might as well say "screw it" and start all over again next week. The problem isn't that a person can't treat themselves or indulge in something every now and then. Rather, it's that each of our acts can set a precedent for what's to follow.

This means you have to be careful in what you do, even if you have the best intentions, to not let it take you down the wrong path. This is why it's important to ask, "What direction will this act take me? What is the long term effect of engaging in this type of behavior?" This isn't to say one has to be perfect or absolutely strict in everything they do, it just means you need to be aware of how any act aligns you to a set of future behavior. Acts must be seen as part of a bigger picture.

You must weigh not only the immediate outcomes of an action, but also consider the path on which that act sets you.

The good news is, seemingly insignificant acts, like taking small steps to better your life, can compound over time. This is the focus of the book The Compound Effect by Darren Hardy. Achieving anything worthwhile will depend on daily, consistent effort and practice. Making one tiny adjustment in the direction of an airplane may seem like an insignificant act, but over the long haul it can mean ending up in an entirely different city.

Closing Thoughts

To close this book, I'd like to leave you with one of the most important concepts I've learned when it comes to getting unstuck, and that is this – success is about *striving*. You're going to screw up plenty of times and make a hell of a lot of mistakes, and that's OK. To this day I sometimes still find myself failing to act upon what I know I need to do, but the reason why I'm able to get out of it is because I can catch myself and get back on track.

While writing this book, resistance took me out tons of times. I got distracted. I worried about things I didn't need to worry about. I didn't always produce my best work. I probably took longer to do things than was necessary. However, in the end, here you are reading it. The reason is that no matter what happened, I knew how to pick myself up and keep going.

"Courage doesn't always roar. Sometimes courage is the little voice at the end of the day that says, 'I'll try again tomorrow.'" – Mary Anne Radmacher

Whenever I'm feeling stuck, my question is "what's one thing I can do right now to align myself to the principles I know?"

Whenever you make the effort to better your life by applying what you've learned in this book, resistance *will* show up. It may make you feel overwhelmed. It may make things feel hopeless. It may make you think that you can't actually make a difference in your life or the world in general, and that you're better off doing nothing. It knows your greatest weakness and will use that against you. You may get knocked down and feel too weak to get back up. This is the game of resistance, and it only wins if you *stay* down. You can always get back up. You can always keep striving. You can always break through whatever is keeping you stuck.

Knowing that you're going to get knocked down, give yourself permission to be OK with that, while making a commitment to always get back up - fast. That's all that really matters. And if you ever need a helping hand to pull yourself up, remember that I'm here for you.

Derek Doepker

Enjoy This Book?

You've made it through the book! Great job! You've already shown your commitment to learn, but remember, true knowledge is applied knowledge. So get out there and make use of this life changing information. If you have any questions, please contact me at derek@derekdoepker.com and I will be glad to assist.

With this book, I wanted to create something that was worth at least 10x as much as I charge for it. So what's my motivation? What do I want? I want you apply it, change your life, and pay it forward by helping others by sharing these tips and resources with them.

The first way to pay it forward is by writing a review of this book to let others know of the benefits you've got from it. This will not only help others better their lives, but it is also incredibly rewarding for me to know how my work has impacted you as well as any ways I can improve.

You can leave a review by going to http://derekdoepker.com/stuck

Thank you!

Derek Doepker

36936273R00089

Made in the USA
Middletown, DE
18 November 2016